The
401(k)
Owner's Manual

The
401(k)
Owner's Manual

A blueprint for building and maintaining
an elite 401(k) plan for your employees

SCOTT EVERHART, CFP®, AIF®
BRIAN HANNA, AIF®
WITH ROBERT SHWAB, CEBS

THE 401(K) OWNER'S MANUAL

iUniverse books may be ordered through booksellers or by contacting:

iUniverse
1663 Liberty Drive
Bloomington, IN 47403
www.iuniverse.com
1-800-Authors (1-800-288-4677)

Because of the dynamic nature of the Internet, any web addresses or links contained in this book may have changed since publication and may no longer be valid. The views expressed in this work are solely those of the author and do not necessarily reflect the views of the publisher, and the publisher hereby disclaims any responsibility for them.

Any people depicted in stock imagery provided by Thinkstock are models, and such images are being used for illustrative purposes only.
Certain stock imagery © Thinkstock.

ISBN: 978-1-5320-1765-0 (sc)
ISBN: 978-1-5320-1769-8 (hc)
ISBN: 978-1-5320-1766-7 (e)

Library of Congress Control Number: 2017905093

Print information available on the last page.

iUniverse rev. date: 06/16/2017

Authors' Note

The authors believe the recommendations and programs presented in this book will assist plan sponsors to design and operate an optimally performing retirement plan and to adopt processes that improve plan sponsors' ability to satisfy their fiduciary responsibilities. The authors have many years of experience in this field as plan advisors and plan administrators. However, while we discuss common understandings and practical use of ERISA and IRS regulations, we are not attorneys and do not intend to provide legal advice. Accordingly, we advise plan sponsors and plan fiduciaries to consult their legal counsel and tax experts prior to making amendments to their plans or implementing any of the programs discussed herein.

To our families, friends, and colleagues who make life wonderful and bring us joy and fascination in all their diverse ways. And to our American free enterprise system that allows us to innovate, work, create, and trade with our fellow citizens in the pursuit of happiness.

Contents

Preface

*T*he *401(k) Owner's Manual* is your blueprint to design and build an elite 401(k) plan. It is intended to educate and provide practical recommendations for plan sponsors, including business owners and corporate managers with responsibility for establishing and maintaining plans, as well as for engaged participants who may participate in plan committees or take an interest in the design and operation of their plan. If your organization is a 501(c)(3) not-for-profit agency, foundation, or private school, *The 401(k) Owner's Manual* is applicable in almost all respects to ERISA 403(b) plans, especially the fiduciary practices.

We will show you how a participant-directed 401(k) plan can lower costs, improve investments, and provide personalized retirement planning and investment advice to employees—all with minimal fiduciary risk to the employer. You can offer a plan that employees see as a highly prized benefit and that prepares them for a secure and comfortable retirement.

Plan sponsors can consult *The 401(k) Owner's Manual* to understand the components of their plan and to avoid the plan weaknesses that lead to employee complaints and DOL investigations. This book will help professionals and providers to look beyond their specific role or service silo and better assist plan sponsors in maintaining a best-in-class plan. The perfect plan may not exist, because for most firms the plan represents a compromise between costs, benefits, and operations. However, you can compare your plan design and functions to the standards we promulgate here, and you will learn best practices to govern your plan to protect fiduciaries and prepare participants for retirement.

We three authors combine more than sixty years of retirement plan experience in every facet of the industry and are uniquely qualified to offer independent and objective analysis. As plan advisors and consultants with the firm of Everhart Advisors, we have no proprietary or commercial interest of any kind in the maintenance or selection of any particular investment, platform, or product. Our clients are business owners, chief financial officers, and human resources managers who serve as fiduciaries of retirement plans in a wide variety of professional, manufacturing, service, and health care businesses, as well as not-for-profit organizations.

Founded in 1995 and recognized as one of the Top 100 advisory firms in the country, Everhart Advisors is an independent retirement plan advisory firm, providing a comprehensive suite of services to enhance qualified retirement plans, including fiduciary protection, investment due diligence, participant education and advice, provider benchmarking, advanced plan design, ERISA compliance, cost control, and fee transparency.

In 2007, the firm began presenting plan sponsor workshops as a source of fiduciary education for the public. These semiannual workshops offer plan sponsors and fiduciaries a forum to gain increased understanding of the vital role they play, the responsibilities they have, the impact of their decisions, and the best practices to employ. Everhart's workshops host a representative from the Department of Labor, with other contributors, including ERISA attorneys, plan auditors, benefits specialists, economists, and investment managers.

The motivation and confidence to write *The 401(k) Owner's Manual* comes after many years in which we successfully implemented our advice into practice. The result is this collection and explication of our best practices, along with several detailed stories of how we helped plan sponsors achieve dramatic improvements.

Visit us at www.everhartadvisors.com to learn more about Everhart Advisors.

Introduction

Why Is It Important to Get It Right regarding Your 401(k) Plan?

Many employers understand the need for and value of sponsoring a retirement plan for employees. However, they are satisfied just to have a 401(k) plan, and about any plan will do. They may assume the plan does not contribute in any direct way to the profitability of the company, attracting or servicing customers, developing new products, or sales and marketing. Your 401(k) plan may be far down the list of business priorities. Perhaps you have not heard or seen any complaints about the 401(k). So, beyond your legal obligations, why devote your time and energy to evaluate and improve the plan?

In the eyes of employees, the quality of the plan features and services is a direct reflection of the quality of your company. Think about the qualities you want your plan to exemplify to employees: efficient, reliable, accurate, innovative, service focused, cost effective. Your 401(k) plan provides an opportunity to reinforce these very qualities and values. Successful companies and leaders understand that employees who feel their company cares about them will transmit that care to their customers. Your company's plan also highlights other positive qualities about employees themselves. Those who are forward thinking and diligent in planning their financial future tend to show those qualities toward their employer and customers.

The 401(k) plan has a very high profile in the workplace. With quarterly statements, a website, and 24-7 mobile account access, employees are reminded frequently about this employee benefit. Moreover, with a major portion of the assets being payroll-deducted contributions from wages and salary, employees are highly aware that the plan assets are entrusted to your care and decisions.

Before the advent of the 401(k) plan, employers offered traditional pension or profit-sharing plans funded solely by employer contributions. Some of these older plans allowed for after-tax employee contributions. The 401(k) section of the Internal Revenue Code became effective in 1980 and allowed employees to defer compensation and shelter taxes on their contribution to the profit-sharing plan. Since the first 401(k) plan features appeared in the early 1980s, 401(k) retirement plans are now the primary vehicle for accumulation of retirement assets for an entire generation of workers and reached $6.5 trillion of assets in 2015. These plans have been at least as important as IRAs in helping individuals save for retirement in a tax-advantaged way.

Yet 401(k) plans have been the focus of complaints from vocal academic and political opinion makers, and these complaints have made their way into the media and in front of your employees. Common themes of these complaints, which have recently appeared before the federal courts in a flood of participant lawsuits, are that the plans are overpriced, the plans include proprietary investments that have not been well vetted, and fiduciaries have neglected substantial conflicts of interest and failed in their duty to monitor investments and vendors. Other critics lament the change away from employer-directed investments to participant investment selection, and argue that the government should play an even larger role in providing retirement income.

Beyond reinforcing corporate culture and values, the 401(k) plan may also have a significant impact on the bottom line for your company in terms of productivity, career management, and medical insurance costs. Companies face the problem of superannuation—referring to things or people that are out of date. One of the highest costs to a business is the employee who needs to retire but does not have the financial resources to do so. Beyond the direct compensation and benefit costs, employers face possible declines in performance by older employees, along with lower morale and decreased motivation among younger employees whose career advancement is delayed. By helping employees accumulate retirement savings, companies allow employees at retirement age to start a new and enjoyable phase of life.

Here is a summary of the topics covered in each chapter:

Chapter 1 discusses the key elements of every plan and how they may be configured in your plan and in the 401(k) marketplace in general.

Chapter 2 explains the specialized knowledge and functions of a plan advisor as distinct from a general financial or investment advisor. If you do not know who the advisor for your plan is, it might be you!

Chapter 3 covers the main responsibilities you signed up for when you became a plan sponsor or fiduciary, why you need to think about fiduciary due diligence and protection, and ways to maximize that protection.

Chapter 4 refers to the set of plan provisions (the rules of the plan) you may customize to achieve the goals you have set for your plan within your overall employee benefits package.

Chapter 5 covers the various cost structures and shell games found in 401(k) plans and how to control those costs.

Chapter 6 covers the process for selecting, monitoring, and changing the service providers, such as the recordkeeper or administrator, for your plan.

Chapter 7 covers the investment due diligence process of creating the menu of investments from which participants choose to invest their monies, and monitoring those investments. We also discuss our view of active versus passive investment management.

Chapter 8 discusses effective employee education and engagement to provide the motivation and information that employees need to formulate their personal retirement goals and plan. We discuss the three types of investors that we encounter regularly—passive, engaged, and active—and focus on behaviors and tools to improve their investment outcomes.

Chapter 9 shows how four plan sponsors with fiduciary concerns and problems made changes to their plans to reduce risks and improve outcomes for participants.

Chapter 1
Components of Every 401(k) Plan

What are the moving parts in your plan? You may not know the components of a 401(k) plan, or, at this point, maybe you are unable to identify them. The terminology in our industry is often misunderstood and misapplied. Jargon like plan administrator, trustee, custodian, recordkeeper, and TPA are often used interchangeably, and communication is confusing, with some of your service providers using different terms to refer to each other. Providers that offer 401(k) services in a bundled product to businesses may function in multiple roles or even all the roles. This only adds complexity to an already confusing structure that lacks transparency. Therefore, we try to clear up the confusion by focusing on the functions that occur within every plan. As shown in the list below, every 401(k) and ERISA 403(b) plan shares these seven essential components. They may operate as separate or combined entities.

401(k) and ERISA 403(b) Plan Components

- plan sponsor
- plan and trust document
- recordkeeping
- compliance and administration

- custodian/trustee
- investment menu
- plan advisor

The *plan sponsor* is the employer offering the retirement plan to its employees and is the responsible party for the plan's design and operation. The plan sponsor is most often the *plan administrator* and the primary *fiduciary*, which are ERISA legal terms we cover in more detail in the next chapter. A plan sponsor may also be a union, trade, or professional association that establishes and operates the plan on behalf of its member employers. Often the plan sponsor will be referred to or requested to sign documents as "trustee" of the plan. Sometimes an individual at the employer plan sponsor is designated also as the trustee responsible for financial statements and filings, but mostly, the use of the term of trustee survives from the era when common trust law was applied to retirement plans.

The *plan and trust document* establishes the plan as its own separate legal entity, and, if it is a qualified plan document according to the Internal Revenue Service (IRS), it provides the tax-deferred advantages of the plan. The plan may apply for and receive its own federal tax identification (EIN) number, although this is not required. Usually, the plan and trust is identified by the EIN of the plan sponsor.

The plan document sets forth the rules of the plan, referred to as plan provisions, which govern the terms and requirements for eligibility, participation, types and amount of contributions, vesting ownership of company-provided benefits, withdrawal, and distributions. Many employers confuse the plan document with the *group annuity contract* or *provider contract*. Those are funding or service contracts that govern the rules between the plan and the insurance company or investment provider. The plan document governs rules between the plan sponsor and the employees. Many of the rules that govern retirement plans are set by the federal employee benefits law and regulation under ERISA, the Employee Retirement Income Security Act. Also, the Internal Revenue Code includes the Section 401 in which paragraphs (a) and (k) allow tax advantages for retirement and 401(k) plans. Therefore, both the Department of Labor and the Internal Revenue Service have jurisdiction over retirements, which is why they both issue regulations and conduct their own audits, exams, and investigations.

However, within the parameters of the IRS and DOL regulations, the employer has many choices of plan provisions. Most plans use a boilerplate, preapproved IRS document, referred to as a prototype, in which the IRS allows the plan sponsor to tailor plan provisions according to a checklist of IRS-approved options. The first section of the prototype plan document is referred to as the Adoption Agreement and contains the checklist and menu of provisions selected by the plan sponsor. The remaining sections of the document codify all the required provisions. Your vendor has submitted to the IRS for preapproval all the boilerplate language and the menu of design choices available for employer selection.

There are many advantages to using a prototype document. It is less expensive and easier to maintain with updates and amendments. Most recordkeepers and providers are able to explain and administer the common provisions. Typically, the prototype document is provided to the plan sponsor by the plan recordkeeper or third-party administrator (TPA), and the plan sponsor does not hire an attorney to draft the document or maintain amendments. If the employer uses the checkbox options within the prototype, they can assume that the form of the plan document (assuming it is signed and timely amended as required) will be acceptable in the event of an examination by the IRS.

When plan sponsors want more flexibility to customize the rules of their plan, for example tiered or varied benefit formulas, or special limitations on eligibility, they may use a *volume submitter* or *individually designed plan document*. These are typically provided by an ERISA attorney, who can advise the employer on customized language that will be acceptable to the DOL and IRS.

These customized documents should be submitted to the IRS for a favorable determination letter, which assures the plan sponsor that the provisions (at least as written) qualify the plan contributions and assets for the desired tax-deferral advantages.

Whichever entity issues your plan document will also prepare a summary plan description (SPD) per the detailed requirements of the Department of Labor. The plan sponsor is responsible for seeing that the SPD and future modifications are distributed to both participants and employees who may become eligible.

The *custodian* and *directed trustee* functions are often combined and synonymously referred to as the trust, trustee, corporate trustee, or directed trustee. The custodian is the financial institution that holds title to the plan assets and provides for receipt and disbursement of monies and for the purchase and sale of investments. In plans funded by mutual funds, the assets are actually held at the mutual fund company. When you, as a participant, request an investment change from one fund to another, your request typically is routed to the recordkeeper through their website and then to the custodian/trustee who relays the buy and sell orders to the mutual fund company. *Ultimately, your choice of custodian determines the list of available investment options, which may be as few as three or as many as twenty thousand.*

The plan document states that the assets must be kept "in trust" as separate from the assets of the company and held "in custody" under the name of the plan for the benefit of the participants of the trust. Just as if you were to establish a personal trust for a child as the beneficiary, the participants are beneficiaries of the 401(k) trust.

The custodian (or directed trustee, in situations where the directed trustee serves as custodian too) reports on financial transactions in the plan and issues an annual consolidated asset and income statement. If your plan has a custodian but not a directed trustee, then an individual fiduciary such as the owner of the company is the trustee and is responsible for the accuracy of the financial statements. We recommend in all cases that the plan sponsor use a directed trustee, also referred to as a corporate trustee—that is, a financial institution that provides custody and also serves as the named trustee. When a directed trustee controls the distribution of assets, plan participants receive an extra degree of protection that plan assets are used solely to pay benefits to participants and beneficiaries as allowed under the plan document. There is usually no cost for the directed trustee service, and it allows for a limited-scope audit for plans with over one hundred account balances, which is less expensive than a full-scope audit. Insurance companies, banks, trust companies, and brokerage accounts may serve as custodians. Note that the group annuity contract serves as the "trust" for a 401(k) plan or 403(b) annuity that is underwritten by an insurance company.

The *recordkeeper* processes and maintains participant account and transaction records, processes contributions and distributions, and receives the payroll and census information. The recordkeeper receives requests and approvals from the plan sponsor and participants and forwards instructions to the custodian. As the vendor providing quarterly statements, participant and plan websites, and service call center, the recordkeeper is the entity you might commonly refer to as the "administrator" of your plan. In a bundled 401(k), the recordkeeper may even provide all the other essential components of the plan such as plan design and documents, compliance, reporting, notices, investment menu selection, and in-house service and advisory staff.

The recordkeeper has a major and sometimes final influence over the plan investment menu. In chapter 6, "Vendor Management and Benchmarking," we comment on how the recordkeeping function is sold and delivered through different business and service models. There are over one hundred providers, from banks, insurance companies, HR and payroll providers, brokerage firms, mutual funds, and pure recordkeeping companies. Each has a unique approach and value proposition. They differ in their document and ERISA capabilities, education and communications, investment flexibility, and technology.

The core recordkeeping function is to track and report the type of contributions and activity in participant accounts. Recordkeepers use the term *sources*, which means the type of contribution. A plan could have the following eight or more contribution sources to be maintained in plan records:

(1) Employee salary reduction 401(k) contributions
(2) Age fifty salary reduction catch-up contributions
(3) Roth 401(k) contributions
(4) Rollover contributions from a prior plan
(5) Employer matching contributions
(6) Employer Safe Harbor contributions
(7) Employer profit-sharing contributions
(8) Qualified nonelective contributions used to avoid or correct discrimination test failures

Because recordkeeping and trust functions must be closely coordinated to function effectively, such as processing a participant loan, the custodian / directed trustee is often a standard service component included with bundled recordkeeping and investment providers. Either a captive trust company owned by the recordkeeper provides the service, or the recordkeeper has integrated a custodian/trust company with its product offering to the plan sponsor. If the recordkeeping and trust functions are not bundled or closely integrated, you will see slower payments and less flexibility in the timing of distributions and exchanges. We see this effect with regional or lower-tier recordkeeping operations.

Compliance and administration (third-party administrator, or TPA) services are essential to satisfy the reporting, notice, and administrative services required by the plan document and the regulatory agencies. When these services are provided by an entity separate from the recordkeeper, the vendor is referred to as a TPA, or third-party administrator. The annual Form 5500 and attached schedules are examples of these services. The annual ADP/ACP discrimination tests for contributions and the top-heavy test of key employees' assets are parts of this service component, which also includes the proliferation of notices that have spread like weeds through the plan administration calendar. Typically, your recordkeeper or TPA will prepare and/or furnish a completed notice or template, and the plan sponsor will be responsible for the distribution of some or all of the notices. Some notices can be delivered by e-mail, and some provider service packages include notice and enrollment fulfillment services, but the oversight is the plan sponsor's responsibility. In a bundled package of services, the recordkeeper provides the compliance and administration services, as well as the plan document.

As part of an unbundled contract with a recordkeeper, an independent third-party administrator (TPA) may provide the compliance and administrative services separately from the other entities, and thereby provides the plan document, summary plan description, and other ERISA-required notices and communications.

In our plan consultations, we are frequently asked, "Do you recommend fully bundled or unbundled service using a TPA?" Our emphasis is always on value, and the decision needs to pass the prudence test by the plan sponsor. Our default recommendation is to use a fully bundled service where the recordkeeper provides the document, compliance, and administrative services, unless the TPA can demonstrate their value.

Traditionally, we saw TPAs process reports already done or capable of being processed at the recordkeeper. This situation added a layer of expense without adding value. Where a plan sponsor is satisfied with a fully bundled situation, we are very reluctant to add a TPA to the plan provider mix.

However, we see the TPA add value in several situations. The employer may not have resources in-house to interact on a regular and reliable basis with the recordkeeper. In some companies, the owner or a partner may have this responsibility, and there is comfort in having a local firm provide a more "concierge" type service and worth the extra cost for the extra support.

We also find real TPA value in plan design, especially in a plan where the tax benefits to the owners/partners are a paramount design objective, often referred to as advanced plan design. Such plan designs may require complex data manipulation and use actuarial calculations to maximize owner contributions within a combined 401(k) and profit-sharing plan. We expect an unbundled TPA to provide an additional level of oversight and consultation in a complex plan design, above the routine services of a bundled recordkeeper. A TPA can also consult on advanced plan designs such as cash balance and defined benefit plans.

The *investment menu* in a 401(k) plan is the filtered list of choices available to a participant from which he or she chooses how to allocate contributions in his or her individual account. The plan sponsor has the ultimate authority and responsibility for determining the investment menu, which might range from virtually unlimited, such as individual self-directed brokerage accounts where each employee selects any investment available from a brokerage firm, to a limited menu of money market, stock, and bond funds.

A key question for the plan sponsor: who or what is determining or influencing the investment menu in your plan? A wide variety of products, services, and provider arrangements influence the investment menu. Here is a review of the most common:

- Group annuity contracts offered through insurance companies combine the recordkeeping and trust/custodian services and construct a list of the investment options that are available to the plan sponsor, who in turn may further limit or select the investments that are offered to employees. The investment options may include public mutual funds, separate investment accounts managed by the insurance company, or subadvised separate accounts using outside investment managers selected by the insurance company. Examples include Principal, Lincoln, Nationwide, Transamerica, and John Hancock. The term *separate account* is derived from insurance company operations to indicate a variable investment account that is separate from the general account of the insurance company and therefore not subject to the claims of policyholders.

- A mutual fund company that also serves as the recordkeeper may offer limited custodian services of only the proprietary mutual funds managed by that firm, or may include outside mutual fund offerings. Examples include Fidelity, Vanguard, and T. Rowe Price.
- Independent recordkeepers are dedicated solely to 401(k) plan services, and they are agnostic and "open architecture" as to investment choices, where as many as 20,000 mutual funds, collective trusts, separate accounts, or ETFs may be available. Examples include Ascensus and Newport.
- The payroll and human resource companies have separate in-house retirement divisions and cross-sell to their corporate clientele. ADP and Paychex are examples in this category.
- Brokerage accounts are custodial arrangements only and do not include recordkeeping or compliance services. Individual accounts for each participant allow for the purchase and sale of individual securities or any fund traded on the brokerage platform. TD Ameritrade or Charles Schwab Brokerage accounts are examples. These arrangements are prevalent at smaller professional and medical practices. However, we rarely see new arrangements of this type due to lack of efficiencies.
- Bank trust operations typically offer open architecture investment options and may use an in-house TPA operation for a fully bundled service. A bank trust officer will usually serve as the plan advisor. Examples include JP Morgan Chase, Wells Fargo, BMO, and Fifth Third Bank.

The *retirement plan advisor* is a person or corporate entity who leads and coordinates plan service providers and vendors, oversees communication programs, provides due diligence, guidance, and support in selecting and monitoring investment options, evaluates contract terms and fees, and assists or explicitly serves in meeting fiduciary responsibilities. Everhart Advisors is a retirement plan advisor, for example. This is the specialty of our firm, to provide independent plan advisory services.

A *bona fide* plan advisor for a qualified retirement plan has specialized knowledge of ERISA and will consult with the plan sponsor to identify needs and objectives and assist with plan design; assist with vendor management; provide tools and advice to assist with plan compliance and fiduciary requirements; draft an investment policy statement; and meet regularly with plan fiduciaries to review plan operations and outcomes. In the next chapter, we will detail the services you should expect from a qualified, independent retirement plan advisor.

Action Items

- ✓ Identify the persons or companies providing each of the essential components of your plan and determine which components are bundled or unbundled.
- ✓ Determine the type of document used by your plan— prototype or customized.
- ✓ Compare the range and type of investments available from different recordkeeping business models.

Chapter 2

What Should I Expect from My Retirement Plan Advisor?

The decision to engage a retirement plan advisor for ongoing service, and the selection of the person or firm, will determine the destiny of your plan. If your company does not hire a retirement plan advisor, then, essentially, the fiduciaries at the plan sponsor are serving in this role. It is also common for us to find that a plan without an advisor is paying advisory compensation costs through implicit contract or investment fund expenses but not receiving the services. That is the worst of all scenarios.

As you read onward in our *401(k) Owner's Manual*, you will see that the plan advisor will be responsible for assuring the reasonable cost and quality of plan services, assisting the plan sponsor in meeting the rigorous fiduciary standards of ERISA, maximizing fiduciary protections, and driving plan goals and participant outcomes.

As a firm dedicated to serving as retirement plan advisors, we come to this topic with an obvious bias in favor of the need of an independent, objective retirement plan specialist. And we are proud to be included among the elite consulting firms serving plan sponsors with care, prudence, and specialized knowledge. We also speak with twenty years of measurable results and a real passion expressed in our simple mission statement: Preparing Participants, Protecting Fiduciaries.

The term "plan advisor" is often ill defined or loosely applied. Many players in the financial industry serve or appear to serve as the plan advisor, and plan sponsors frequently misunderstand this role. A 401(k) or 403(b) plan or plan investments may be sold by a benefits consultant, financial planner, stock broker, financial advisor, insurance agent, bank trust officer, registered investment advisor, accountant, third-party administrator (TPA), or by the recordkeeper directly through their in-house sales representative. In a bundled 401(k) product with an insurance company, bank, or mutual fund firm, the provider may be acting in the plan advisor role. There are inherent conflicts of interest that complicate your fiduciary tasks when your recordkeeper or TPA is also your plan advisor. In some of these situations, compensation is received without genuine advisory services being provided.

There is common difficulty and confusion among plan sponsors in distinguishing between the retirement plan advisor and an investment advisor. A professional retirement plan advisor is a specialist who combines investment expertise, plan compliance, plan design, and employee education programs with process management capabilities. While often thought of by plan sponsors as the "investment advisor," the plan advisor specialist is familiar with the ever-increasing complexity of 401(k) plan compliance and governance. Engaging plan advisor consulting firms familiar with ERISA and dedicated to the retirement plan space is now considered best practice.

An investment advisor offers investment portfolio management and investment manager due diligence only and does not specialize in 401(k) plan processes or participant retirement readiness. In our view, an investment advisor focus is too narrow to assist and add the necessary value in the role of retirement plan advisor. The industry training and credential programs differ for each of these professionals. The top investment advisors have earned the esteemed chartered financial analyst (CFA) designation sponsored by the CFA Institute, or the highly regarded certified financial planner (CFP) credential that is granted by the Certified Financial Planner Board of Standards, Inc. A CFA is qualified to manage a mutual fund or construct a portfolio of individual equity and fixed-income securities. The CFP training and experience requirements focus on broad financial planning and wealth management for individuals and families.

By contrast, retirement plan advisors are trained and credentialed through programs that focus on the fiduciary responsibilities under ERISA. The accredited investment fiduciary (AIF) granted by fi360, Inc. reflects knowledge and competency in the area of fiduciary studies and is the most common plan advisor credential. The International Foundation of Employee Benefit Plans sponsors a joint education program with the Wharton School and offers the Certified Employee Benefit Specialist (CEBS). The Chartered Retirement Plans Specialist (CRPS) is another plan advisor training program sponsored by the College for Financial Planning. Another useful credential for working with participants is the certified behavioral finance analyst available through training at the Allianz Institute. In addition, a variety of very well-respected retirement plan credentials for advisors, actuaries, and administrators are available through training programs run by ASPAA, the American Society of Pension Professionals & Actuaries.

Plan sponsors often do not pay much attention to plan advisor training and credentials, but we believe they should, given the array of "financial advisor" labels representing disparate skill sets. Credentials are one way of differentiating a dilettante from a specialist. Business colleges and MBA programs do not train graduates in this specialty. You cannot call up the local college and ask to interview the new 401(k) graduates.

A stockbroker, insurance agent, or financial advisor (technically referred to as a *registered representative* under FINRA) is focused mainly on the sales process and early stage consultations. They are usually familiar with several vendors and products but do not expect to accept fiduciary responsibility or provide ongoing fiduciary guidance or plan design assistance. The registered representative is commissioned and will be limited to offer only the products and investments approved by their supervising brokerage firm, called a broker-dealer. The investment funds held by the plan will make payments to the brokerage firm, which in turn will keep a portion for broker-dealer overhead and pay out a portion to the individual or group you know as your broker. He or she may receive as a little as 40 percent of the payment made by the plan to the brokerage firm dealer. With very few exceptions, the plan sponsor will not be able to develop a low-cost plan through a commissioned broker.

TPAs and some accountants have ERISA expertise but usually lack certified investment expertise and do not deliver comprehensive participant education programs. The all-in-one recordkeeper may offer broad services but has in-born conflicts of interest and is not likely to offer objective advice and benchmarking of their own fees and services. It is worth repeating, as we first pointed out in our chapter 1 discussion, without the oversight by an independent advisor, recordkeepers that also offer their own funds are less likely to recommend replacement of one of their own funds.

An independent plan advisor is not employed by or benefiting as a party-in-interest to any plan vendor or investment. Your independent plan advisor is hired by the plan sponsor on the basis of a written compensation and services agreement. The differentiation from financial generalists is the plan advisor's independence and primary focus on 401(k) plans. As with your legal, tax, or management consultants, the plan advisor should fit in as an extension of your finance and HR departments. Plan advisors should be the first point of contact for plan sponsors when a serious problem or concern arises, and the first source for new ideas, improvements, and developments. Compared with plans that operate with a generalist advisor or do not use an advisor or consultant at all, the plan that engages a specialized retirement plan advisor should expect to enjoy and document better results.

Superior Retirement Outcomes for Participants

Your plan advisor will collaborate with the plan sponsor to set goals for plan participants and measure the retirement readiness progress of participants. Education and communication programs are developed and presented by the plan advisor. We have encountered many plan sponsors who were convinced that employees could not be educated or motivated to participate in a meaningful way in the retirement plan. A skilled plan advisor can overcome employee neglect or inertia and succeed with any participant population. In the last chapter, we document a few such success stories.

Superior Process for Fiduciary Issues

It is well established in ERISA fiduciary law that prudence refers to process, not results. With the help of the plan advisor, the plan sponsor will establish a retirement plan committee that meets regularly to make plan decisions. Meetings give busy executives a forum to hear from the plan advisor about legislation, litigation, and regulations impacting plans and fiduciaries. The plan advisor maintains a fiduciary *briefcase* to document that deliberate and prudent processes are in place to exercise fiduciary responsibilities. Should a future result or policy come under question, the committee can refer back to the rationale at the time of the decision. Committee proceedings are documented in minutes and agendas. If the advisor service contract provides for education services, then those activities should be documented.

Better Plan Designs

The plan advisor should be familiar with your plan provisions and new design ideas to help achieve the plan's objectives within the company's employee benefit budget and will understand the internal administrative costs and resources needed to maintain the plan. As an industry expert, the 401(k) specialist will be familiar and have access to the benchmarking and competitive reports and databases appropriate for comparisons with your plan.

The plan advisor should be reviewing the quarterly plan reports (which might run one hundred pages) and cull out the significant data points and prepare an executive summary for the committee. Plan sponsors consult with their plan advisor on strategies to pass discrimination tests, optimize benefits, and minimize operational risks.

Better Overall Asset Allocation among Plan Participants

Your plan advisor should be an expert in the pros and cons of various asset allocation funds, portfolios, and models and provide useful advice on the most appropriate choices for a particular plan population. As you will see later in our discussion of participant outcomes, the plan advisor can recommend and help implement strategies to improve overall and participant-level asset allocation.

More Reasonable Fees and More Efficient Vendor Management

Plan sponsors should rely on the plan advisor to manual a methodical and statistically valid approach to benchmarking plan expenses, including all sources of plan compensation. Where we have taken over the plan advisor role from a generalist advisor, the total plan costs have usually declined significantly. Plan advisors know where to find and eliminate unnecessary costs. They also can leverage relationships with best-in-class providers to negotiate reduced costs and deliver improved services.

In performing vendor selection and management services on your behalf, plan advisors make site visits to top-tier providers and work through their organizational charts to know and meet key managers and executives at those organizations. This is extremely helpful to the plan sponsor in the selection process and in the event of future serious issues.

When a change in funds or plan providers is warranted, the plan advisor manages the conversion process.

DOL Fiduciary Rule and the "Best Interests" Standard of Care

The plan advisor is also your investment advisor with specialized knowledge and due diligence tools to select and monitor a 401(k) plan investment menu on a continuing basis. At Everhart Advisors, we serve as a designated ERISA fiduciary under the plan for investment purposes. As a registered investment advisor, we serve the plan as an ERISA fiduciary and accept a fiduciary level of responsibility in performing our duties. In the next chapter, we discuss in more depth the differences between the ERISA 3(21) co-fiduciary and 3(38) fiduciary.

Under the fiduciary standard, the advisor is obligated to give objective, prudent advice in the best interests of the plan participants and beneficiaries. The "best interests" requirement is a higher standard than the "suitability" requirement of the traditional broker or registered representative. In the general financial marketplace, an investment recommendation only needs to be "appropriate" for the customer's objectives and financial situation (not necessarily in their best interests) in order to be "suitable."

In April 2016, the Department of Labor issued what is called the DOL Fiduciary Rule, a regulation that expands the definition of a fiduciary and requires investment advisors to accept fiduciary responsibility and adopt the "best interests" standard anytime they are engaged by retirement plan customers to provide advice. Essentially, the DOL holds the financial advisor to the same fiduciary level of prudence and care as the plan sponsor. Employers should note that the rule applies especially to IRA rollovers from the plan. According to the White House Fact Sheet (April 6, 2016) issued on the release of the rule, "any individual receiving compensation for making investment recommendations that are individualized or specifically directed to a particular plan sponsor running a retirement plan (e.g., an employer with a retirement plan), plan participant, or IRA owner for consideration in making a retirement investment decision is a fiduciary." The fiduciary designation requires that the investment advisor offering a recommendation must provide "impartial advice in their client's best interest." Furthermore, the advisor cannot accept any payments creating conflicts of interest unless they qualify for an exemption by making specific disclosures and assurances intended to assure that the customer's interests are protected.

Congress and the president may repeal this rule before it is implemented. Nevertheless, discussion around the rule is instructive for plan sponsors to understand the difference between the two standards.

What Is the Cost for Plan Advisor Services?

Plan advisors typically charge a percentage fee, depending on the size of the plan and number of participants, which ranges from .10 percent to .50 percent of plan assets. The fee is derived from the advisor's estimated staff hours and level of work effort to service the plan participants and fiduciaries. For limited and discrete consulting engagements, advisors may be retained for an hourly fee that may range from $300 to $1,000 per hour, again depending on the staff level assigned to the project.

Larger plans by assets and participant size will encounter more complex service issues. However, as the plan asset size grows, the work of the plan advisor does not necessarily increase proportionately, so ongoing review of the advisor's services and level of effort is prudent and necessary.

When your plan advisor has fiduciary responsibility, he or she cannot cause the plan to engage in a prohibited transaction—that is, an expense that is not necessary. Therefore, it is necessary for the advisor to understand completely which services the plan needs and which services the advisor can provide. Those services that are not utilized by the plan fiduciaries or participants should be carved out from the offering, and the corresponding fees reduced.

Everhart Advisors is a member of the Retirement Plan Advisory Group (RPAG), a national practice support and research group for retirement plan advisors. RPAG recommends that a plan sponsor ask the following questions to gather important information about plan advisor candidates:

- *What percentage of your total assets is from 401(k) plan advisory services and consulting, and how many of your employees are dedicated to your 401(k) plan practice?* Firms that are focused heavily on 401(k) plan consulting tend to offer more comprehensive and consistent services.
- *What are the total qualified plan assets under management of the plan sponsors you serve? How many clients do you serve in each of the following plan asset categories?*

    o   under $5 million
    o $5 million to $20 million
    o $20 to $50 million
    o $50 to $100 Million
    o   over $100 Million

    This figure will indicate the types of clients served by the consulting firm. A consultant who is familiar with plans of your size and demographics may be able to better understand your needs, and deliver more comprehensive services, than firms who lack experience working with plans your size.

- *Is your firm a registered investment advisor?* Only firms that are registered with the SEC and the state in which they operate may call themselves a registered investment advisor. If your firm is a registered investment advisor (RIA), do you accept co-fiduciary status under ERISA? With the acceptance of a co-fiduciary role, your advisor becomes a willing partner with respect to the monitoring and selection of plan investments.

- *Does your firm provide a written retainer agreement or service contract detailing the services that you provide?* Best-practices plan advisors will quantify the frequency and scope of the services they provide.
- *Does your firm disclose all forms of compensation, including commissions, bonus payments, fees, revenue sharing, and other forms of compensation? How is this information disclosed to us?* As a plan sponsor, you have the right and fiduciary obligation to know how much your plan consultant is being paid. This information should be disclosed in advance and readily available for you to review at any time.
- *How much Errors & Omissions insurance does your firm have (per incident and aggregate annual coverage)? How many representatives are covered under this policy?* Per incident coverage is the maximum limit for one specific claim. Aggregate coverage is the maximum total annual claims limit for all representatives covered under the policy.
- *Does your firm or a related firm also offer third-party administrative (TPA) services?* A TPA is a service provider. Plan consultants help plan sponsors hire and retain services providers. Therefore, there is a conflict of interest with firms that are both a TPA and plan consultant.
- *Are the representatives from your firm that will be servicing us on an ongoing basis available for an on-site due diligence interview at your office?* Best-practices consulting firms should be eager to demonstrate their service capabilities and human capital resources to you.
- *Have your investment materials been reviewed by outside legal counsel for compliance with ERISA?* ERISA Section 404(a) details the investment monitoring responsibilities facing plan sponsors. ERISA counsel's review and affirmation of compliance with 404(a) is an indication of a best-practices approach to investment due diligence.
- *What software and research tools do your firm use to prepare investment research reports for plan sponsors?* The

three generally accepted most robust investment research tools are: Zephyr StyleADVISOR, Ibbotson Encore, and MPI Stylus. Other tools such as Morningstar Principia are helpful but provide significantly less meaningful and comprehensive data.

- *How many individuals in your firm are available to provide group or individual employee education meetings for our employees?* Some plan consultants outsource this service completely to the service provider. Firms that have capabilities in this area have a greater ability to customize meaningful employee education solutions for your employees.
- *Please list the qualifications for the person(s) who will be responsible for delivering ongoing service to our plan:*
  o industry experience
  o number of customers serviced in their total block of business
  o percentage of time representatives dedicate to service
- *Will our plan have a dedicated service rep with bottom-line accountability?* Best-practices consulting firms typically have dedicated customer service representatives with bottom-line accountability for the success of your plan.

Finally, you can highlight some of the ideas and issues from this book and ask the plan advisor for their own approach.

Action Items

- ✓ Identify the person or company serving in the role of plan advisor and determine his or her status and capabilities both as a plan fiduciary and as a plan specialist.
- ✓ Define the scope of duties of the plan advisor.
- ✓ Evaluate the fees and services of the plan advisor.
- ✓ Establish and track plan advisor service goals and deliverables.

Chapter 3

Who Is the Fiduciary, and What Does ERISA Require?

All from tuppence, prudently
fruitfully, frugally invested
In the ... Fidelity Fiduciary Bank!
　　　　　　—From *Mary Poppins*, Walt Disney

Maybe your first recollection of the term "fiduciary" was as a child watching the Walt Disney movie *Mary Poppins* and the actor Dick Van Dyke playing the parsimonious president of the Fidelity Fiduciary Bank. Real-life fiduciaries of our generation may recall the actor in a three-piece pinstriped suit, with a gold pocket watch and white beard advising the children to invest and spend their two pence, or "tuppence," wisely and *prudently*.

If you or someone you know has served as a volunteer or board member for a charitable, religious, educational, or human services organization, you can understand that a fiduciary has a duty and obligation—under the law and morally—to govern the assets and operation of the organization in a way to optimize benefits to the beneficiaries and preserve the organization for future beneficiaries. *Govern the plan as though it were a charity where you are the board president.*

Under ERISA Section 404(a) (1) (B), a particular fiduciary

definition and duty apply to employee benefit plans: anyone who is a trustee, sponsor or otherwise exercises any authority or control over any type of employee benefit plan is a fiduciary. "The fiduciary should act with the care, skill, prudence, and diligence under the circumstances then prevailing that a prudent man acting in a like capacity and familiar with such matters would use in the conduct of an enterprise of like character and with like aims."

You are a fiduciary if you have the authority, control, and/ or effective influence as to the design and administration of the plan. Business owners, CEOs, CFOs, HR managers, and 401(k) plan committee members may likely be fiduciaries. Under ERISA, fiduciaries have personal liability for assets in the company's retirement plan. Unlike most other corporate responsibilities, under ERISA, you (and your assets) can be held personally liable for plan losses due to your failure to act prudently as a plan fiduciary.

If your organization maintains a 403(b) plan covered by ERISA, the plan and the fiduciaries will be subject to the ERISA standard of care and responsibility. Because a not-for-profit agency with a volunteer and unpaid board of directors has a far different governing structure compared to the typical private company, it is even more important to ensure that plan fiduciary duties, roles, and procedures are clearly defined and documented.

An ERISA fiduciary has a high level of responsibility under ERISA and Department of Labor regulations to faithfully operate the plan according to its provisions, to diligently conduct all functions and duties, and to maintain and invest plan assets for the exclusive benefit of the participants and with the care, prudence, and skill of a person with similar trust responsibilities and familiar with such matters. This is often referred to as the "prudent expert" standard. Fiduciary oversight applies also to administrative determinations concerning eligibility, enrollment, hours of service and vesting calculations, contribution calculations and funding, loans and withdrawals, and beneficiary claims. ERISA legal experts stress the critical requirement of process and documentation to satisfy fiduciary obligations.

If you are a finance executive responsible for investments, you should note that the management of plan investments under the "prudent expert" standard is a higher legal standard than the prudent person standard for corporate investments. The fact that a plan sponsor may have acted with good intentions or in good faith is no defense if their conduct did not meet the expert standard. The standard applies to the trust as a whole rather than to individual investments. No particular investment is inherently prudent or imprudent.

Who Is Not a Fiduciary?

Unless you have a specific and written agreement that delegates and accepts particular fiduciary duties and responsibilities, the common understanding is that your providers are not fiduciaries. By the term "providers," we include consultants, advisors, brokers, recordkeepers, mutual fund companies, insurance companies, banks, or insurance agents who may provide service to your plan. Their contracts or service agreements specify that they do not accept fiduciary responsibility. There are situations where a person rejects the fiduciary label but acts in a way that creates fiduciary responsibility. An ERISA attorney can advise who is a fiduciary under your plan. Under the 2016 DOL Fiduciary Rule, all plan advisors must adapt a fiduciary level of care, and this will be a mandated responsibility.

A best practice is to identify the plan fiduciaries and document their selection and appointment in a board resolution or committee charter, along with the written service agreement with outside fiduciaries. Retain these documents in a fiduciary briefcase.

What Should You Be Doing as a Fiduciary?

Our client Carol is an HR manager who attended one of our DOL fiduciary workshops. Sometime later, she was hired at a new enterprise and was assigned responsibility for managing the 401(k) retirement plan for employees. She understood that she was one of the fiduciaries for the plan. However, it seemed to Carol that the 401(k) plan recordkeeper had selected investments, advised on the plan design, and was providing all the compliance and administrative services. She wondered, *What exactly should I be doing as a fiduciary?*

As an employer and manager (and as a participant yourself), you will be interested in plan results—growth of assets, investment returns, plan participation—and that is one of the main purposes of this book. Your plan providers (see the Plan Components above) will perform the tasks and provide the documents and records needed under ERISA and IRS regulations. However, from the sole point of view of an ERISA fiduciary, you are interested in prudent processes to oversee these important tasks:

- Maintain the tax-qualified status by ensuring the plan document and amendments are signed and up to date, and ensure the providers are performing the IRS coverage, discrimination, and top-heavy tests and requirements.
- Department of Labor reporting (annual Form 5500 and schedules), disclosures, and notices are completed and distributed.
- Processes and procedures are in place to administer the plan according to the plan document provisions, so that eligibility and vesting is tracked and employees are offered the opportunity to enroll.
- Ensure that contributions are calculated correctly and deposited timely.
- Distributions, loans, and withdrawals are performed correctly.
- Plan information and education materials and tools are made available to employees.
- Investment menu is selected and monitored.
- Ensure that costs for services are reasonable and that those services are necessary.
- Maintain written records of fiduciary governance, decisions, and procedures.

As a plan fiduciary, you are responsible for selecting the vendors who perform these tasks and monitoring their fees and performance on an ongoing basis. A plan fiduciary should maintain internal management reporting and controls and document decisions. If the company has a benefits or 401(k) committee, then the committee secretary should maintain a file of meeting minutes and exhibits.

Starting with plan year 2016, the IRS and DOL will add more specific questions in the annual Form 5500 filing to target their plan audits and examinations. They will be looking for plan documents to be updated with amendments, asking about in-service distributions and reviewing more detail about discrimination tests. A complex plan benefit formula, excess distributions, or lax verification of hardship withdrawals can be a red flag for an IRS audit or a DOL investigation and could lead to employer penalties or fines. In a rare and worst-case scenario, the IRS can withdraw the plan's qualified status, rendering the assets and prior contributions taxable to participants.

Minimizing Fiduciary Investment Risks—
Three Layers of Defense

The following three elements provide essential layers of fiduciary protection as to investment responsibilities under your plan:

1. Section 404(c) of ERISA shields the plan sponsor from participant investment results where special notice, information, and participant-directed plan features are available and delivered to employees.
2. The plan implements and monitors a qualified default investment alternative (QDIA) to shield the plan sponsor from investment results when assets are invested according to a default investment, where an employee has failed to make his or her own investment election.
3. A written investment policy statement (IPS) provides guidance and process for fiduciaries charged with the selection and monitoring of investments.

In its simplest explanation, ERISA Section 404(c) provides that the employee and not the employer is responsible for the results of his or her own investment choices. The case for 404(c) protection is most obvious when comparing profit-sharing and 401(k) plans where the employer directs investments for pooled assets. We continue to see these so-called trustee-directed retirement plans, where the plan's sponsor is a discretionary trustee and assumes all the investment responsibility by managing all or part of the plan assets in a pooled account. The employer, or its designated investment advisor, makes all the investment decisions, and all participants, whether old or young, with aggressive or conservative profiles, are invested in the same investments and share the same allocation.

Although easy for participants, there are serious problems with this "one size fits all" approach. Obviously, not all employees fit the same investor risk profile. Younger employees will generally need more growth; older employees will generally seek more preservation. Moreover, the employer is assuming all the responsibility and risk of investment selections, timing, and allocations. When a participant is eligible and demands a distribution, perhaps unanticipated or at a time of great market volatility, the trustee may need to liquidate long-term investments at an unfavorable moment to the detriment of the remaining participants. For these reasons, the overwhelming majority of 401(k) plans have transitioned to participant investment direction and utilizes the protection of ERISA Section 404(c).

In order to rely on Section 404(c), the plan document must include a provision that the plan is offered to participants on the basis of ERISA Section 404(c), which provides that if a plan with individual accounts allows a participant to exercise control over the investment of his or her account assets, the fiduciary will be relieved of liability for any resulting losses. In the usual practice, this means that where a participant has selected the investments for his or her own account from a plan menu of investments, the employer is not responsible for the investment results.

The Department of Labor has issued 404(c) regulations, which have become the subject of complex legal debate as to their exact meaning and application. However, there is general understanding and widespread practice to administer 404(c) under the following necessary conditions:

- Participants are notified that the plan intends to operate under 404(c) and that the participants exercise investment direction.
- Participants can select from a menu of diversified investments that include at least three options—cash, equity, and fixed income.
- Mutual fund prospectus and informational materials are immediately available (usually by website) and include a general description of the investment objectives and risk and return characteristics of the investment.
- Participants make initial investment elections and are provided the instructions and opportunity to make investment changes.
- Information is provided to participants on investment expenses and particular investment restrictions.

Section 404(c) does not require educational programs, but participants must have access to sufficient information to enable them to make informed investment decisions. Complex investments (such as guaranteed investment contracts or deferred annuities) have a higher informational requirement. We see plan sponsors who fail to provide the 404(c) notice, which is a key item absolutely needed for this protection, and so the notice is one of the items on our compliance checklist. Keep in mind that the 404(c) protection for fiduciaries provides a "safe harbor," assuming that the menu of choices offered to participants is prudent. Section 404(c) does not allow the fiduciary to abdicate his or her duty to monitor the investment menu. The participants are responsible for their selections from the investment menu, but the plan sponsor is still responsible to ensure the investment menu is appropriate. A plan advisor that provides investment advice and accepts fiduciary responsibility under ERISA can provide ongoing recommendations through a prudent process to maintain the investment menu.

Qualified Default Investment Alternative (QDIA)

Perhaps the most important investment decision that a fiduciary will make is the choice of QDIA, which is the second basic layer of fiduciary protection.

There was an uncovered gap in the 404(c) protection for fiduciaries in situations where a participant was enrolled in a plan without making an investment election. This could happen where a participant makes a salary reduction contribution or receives an employer contribution or, in more recent years, where the participant is enrolled "automatically," and their monies are invested pursuant to the default investment. The participant did not elect the investment, and so this becomes a potential employer liability.

The Pension Protection Act of 2006 (PPA of 2006) expanded the fiduciary protection of ERISA 404(c) and offered a solution to the default problem by providing for "qualified default investment alternatives." If specific disclosure and notice requirements are satisfied, the plan fiduciary is not liable for the investment results where participant contributions are invested into a default investment option that has been selected by the plan sponsor.

Traditionally, the money market or fixed interest account served as the default investment. However, under the new legislation, the Department of Labor waded deep into the pool of investment options that might serve as the "qualified" default and declared that a money market or interest account would not suffice as a viable default option beyond the first 120 days of enrollment.

Together, the 404(c) coverage with the QDIA is a cornerstone of fiduciary protection. Now, however, the plan sponsor faces the complicated task of selecting and monitoring the QDIA. Under the DOL regulations, there are three basic types of QDIAs:

1. Target date funds (TDFs) or model portfolios based on a participant's age, expected retirement date, or life expectancy (2025, 2030, 2040 ...) or lifecycle funds or model portfolios based on a risk profile (conservative, moderate, aggressive)
2. A single balanced fund or model portfolio with a risk profile appropriate for participants of the plan as a whole
3. A managed account where the participant's monies are allocated by an investment management advisor or computer model that uses generally accepted investment theories and takes into account information about the participant such as their age, current account balance, contribution rate, and compensation

The advent of the QDIA and DOL rules that encouraged automatic enrollment led to the widespread creation of target date funds by investment companies and wide utilization by plan sponsors. From 2008 to 2015, these target date funds and similar collective trusts accumulated $1.1 trillion of assets. A target date fund is a combination of stock, bond, and cash investments in a mixture (an asset allocation) that changes over time toward a more conservative allocation as the participant approaches the particular target date, based on birth date or expected retirement date. It is common to find fourteen or more different asset classes managed within one fund or portfolio. The gradual change in allocation is referred to as the glide path of the fund. It is generally assumed that the participant will be age sixty-five at the target date. Thus, a forty-year-old in 2020 might select or be defaulted to the 2045 target date fund.

What could be easier for a participant or plan sponsor? With only a date of birth, the participant can be enrolled in a seemingly permanent investment solution.

The target date fund became a media story in the Great Recession starting in 2008, around which time the first wave of participants whose investments were selected by default, including participants within five years or less of retirement, found that their one fund solution had lost 30 percent or more of its value. Plan sponsors learned that not all target date funds were constructed the same way. A 2010 target date fund might use anywhere from 40 percent to 80 percent equities, and glide path adjustments to a conservative allocation might start at age sixty or age seventy. Furthermore, questions arose concerning the choice of managers and funds within the fund and the use of proprietary target date funds. Many 401(k) recordkeepers only offered one or very limited choices of target date funds. Plan advisors noted that one investment company might not have sufficient expertise to manage all the asset classes.

You should also evaluate how participants are making use of the target date funds and whether or not their utilization satisfies the plan sponsor's objectives. A recent survey commissioned by Financial Engines, a web-based participant advice firm, pointed out that among target date fund users, only a quarter (26 percent) report using these one-stop solutions as they were designed by investing all or at least 90 percent of their retirement assets in their age-appropriate target date Fund. The majority of participants continued to select individual funds alongside their target date fund, which they perceived as a single solution lacking manager diversification. (This may or may not be true; some target date funds include diverse management companies assigned to specific asset classes.) Likely, they wanted to avoid "putting all their eggs in one basket" with the target date product. And they may very well be seeking more personalized asset allocation appropriate to their individual risk profile, beyond their assumed retirement age.

Among Everhart Advisors clients, we find that customized target date funds and customized allocation portfolios are more popular with participants and have a higher rate of utilization than the basic target date fund.

In February 2013 in a document entitled "Target Date Retirement Funds—Tips for ERISA Plan Fiduciaries," the Department of Labor issued guidelines for plan sponsors to consider in the selection and monitoring of QDIAs. Target date funds (TDFs) are a particular focus, because they have become the most widely used QDIA, but they are not well understood by plan sponsors or participants. The DOL highlights eight key considerations as a prudent process for QDIA selection and monitoring:

- Establish a process for comparing and selecting TDFs.
- Conduct a periodic review of TDFs.
- Understand the fund (or model's) investments.
- Review fees and investment expenses.
- Examine both proprietary and nonproprietary funds.
- Develop effective employee communications.
- Review independent sources of information to evaluate the TDF and recommendations regarding the selection.
- Document the selection and ongoing review process.

It is clear from the DOL guidance and regulations that the choice of a QDIA is not a one-time event. A variety of analytic tools enables the plan sponsor to compare the asset allocation, glide path, asset diversification, and expenses of target date funds.

Investment Policy Statement

Your third layer of fiduciary defense is the investment policy statement (IPS). This is a written document that governs the fiduciary process for plan investment decisions. The IPS describes the investment menu structure and provides guidelines for fund selection and benchmarks for fund evaluation. The IPS provides the standing rationale behind the fund menu, but it should not be so detailed that it must be updated constantly. It describes the range and type of investments that are permissible, rather than listing specific funds or investment managers. Our objective is to draft the IPS so that it provides guidance but is not so inflexible that it commands action within a narrow range of measurements in response to short-term market volatility.

A written policy should not be a substitute for an engaged and expert-level plan advisor. The plan advisor's periodic fund analysis provides the proof for the IPS. In chapter 1, "Components of Every 401(k) Plan," we noted the possible negative impact of proprietary investments—that is, funds owned or otherwise favored by the recordkeeper or custodian. An IPS combined with an independent, diligent monitoring process ensures that proprietary funds are evaluated neutrally.

Our service engagements as a plan advisor often start with the IPS. Although not a legal requirement, it is one of the first items the DOL will request in an examination. With recent legal developments in cost monitoring, we expect that the investment policy statement will be accompanied by an expense policy statement that describes the procedure for selecting fund share classes and allocating expenses.

Sharing Fiduciary Investment Responsibility

> I now quit altogether public affairs and I lay down
> my burden.
>
> —King Edward VIII,
> December 11, 1936, abdicating the crown

If you do not know the history of King Edward's dilemma, you can see the story in the movie *The King's Speech*, starring Colin Firth. King Edward VIII becomes the only English monarch ever to resign the throne voluntarily. We will not spoil the plot for you, except to say that he had other distractions and an attractive American woman is a part of the story. You might be thinking, *I don't want to be a fiduciary,* and wondering if someone else can take on the responsibility. ERISA has provisions that allow a plan sponsor to share fiduciary responsibility and tasks related to the investment of plan assets. You can limit responsibility and delegate authority. However, unlike King Edward, who turned the reign over to his brother, the plan sponsor cannot abdicate fiduciary responsibility.

A co-fiduciary is a simple and practical way for a plan sponsor to delegate investment fiduciary tasks and share responsibility with a prudent expert. Under Section 3(21) of ERISA, the plan sponsor may engage an investment advisor as a co-fiduciary to provide investment advice regarding plan investments. Most bona fide plan advisors offer a 3(21) service. This assignment does not relieve the plan sponsor of ultimate responsibility, and so the 3(21) advisor is referred to as a "co-fiduciary." Generally, a registered investment advisor (RIA), broker-dealer and registered representative, bank or insurance company may serve in this co-fiduciary role and enters into a written agreement with the plan sponsor. A 3(21) investment advisor is subject to the ERISA fiduciary prudence standards and through prudent process and investment due diligence makes recommendations to the plan sponsor such as the menu of investment options available to participants, asset allocation models, and the selection of the default QDIA.

The advice is nondiscretionary, meaning that the plan sponsor may or may not implement the advice. The 3(21) is only a fiduciary with respect to the advice provided and not regarding other aspects of the plan.

A limited number of plan sponsors have taken delegation a step further by appointing a 3(38) investment manager with full discretionary authority over investment decisions, meaning that the plan sponsor will make no decisions concerning the investment of plan assets that are under control of the 3(38) investment manager. For example, the investment manager would have sole discretion to select the menu of investment options offered to employees. Only an RIA, bank, or insurance company can serve in this role. In our view, the current marketing of 3(38) services implies the complete abdication of employer responsibility. Everhart Advisors will serve in either the 3(21) or 3(38) role. However, be aware that whether using a 3(21) investment advisor or 3(38) investment manager, the plan sponsor still has fiduciary responsibility for the selection and monitoring of these persons or firms, including analysis of the fees and services of the 3(21) or 3(38) advisor. So, the plan sponsor has still not absolved him or herself of liability.

Does a Fiduciary Warranty Provide Shelter from Liability?

For no apparent cost or additional fees, several insurance companies offer a product feature or rider in their group annuity contract referred to as a fiduciary warranty. The warranty offers typically to cover plan sponsor legal costs and damages for ERISA claims based on the provider's selection of investment managers. These warranties are not recognized under ERISA 3(21) and provide limited protection against a very unlikely set of risks. Apparently, the "free" warranty is commensurate with the risk, because in our years of experience, we have never seen a lawsuit or claim against the plan sponsor for the choice of the particular investment managers within a diversified selection of investment options. In other words, plan sponsors are not sued because they selected Mid Cap Value Fund Manager ABC versus Mid Cap Value Fund Manager XYZ.

The risk to the plan sponsor, and it is a risk not covered by the warranty, is the selection of the group annuity product itself and the expenses and contract terms therein.

In 2013, a federal district court in California allowed a class-action lawsuit to proceed against a major insurance provider. In an order regarding a motion to dismiss (not the final court decision), the court criticized the fiduciary warranty included in the group annuity contract. The court held that the participants had a potential prohibited transaction claim that the warranty was a mechanism for the insurance company, as a conflicted party-in-interest, to encourage and subsidize the placement of its own proprietary investment funds. The court also noted that participants in effect paid the cost of the warranty as benefit to the employer.

Regardless of the ultimate disposition of this litigation, we share the concerns of the court and would give very little weight to the value of a fiduciary warranty.

Sharing Fiduciary Administrative Responsibility

Your payroll and HR department can be a source of fiduciary risk and penalties. The IRS and DOL have collected millions of dollars of penalties from plan sponsors—not for investment funds underperforming but for employer errors and omissions in plan administration such as enrollment, vesting and contribution calculations, late remittance of contributions, and various failures to follow the myriad IRS rules and terms of the plan document related to withdrawals and loans. Every DOL examination will review the accuracy and timeliness of payroll remittance. High-risk administrative functions also include the determination of "hardship" requests and failure to obtain spousal approval for distributions to married participants. Many of these functions are dependent on the accuracy of data in your HR and payroll systems.

However, you may be able to share fiduciary responsibility with your plan providers, such as your recordkeeper or TPA firm. Section 3(16) of ERISA defines the "plan administrator" as the person or entity that has authority over plan operations. In single employer plans, this plan administrator is usually you—our reader—the fiduciary at the employer; except in special and clearly defined situations, it is not the recordkeeper or TPA. However, under Section 3(16) of ERISA, the plan sponsor may share administrative fiduciary responsibility or delegate many of these tasks to the TPA or recordkeeper. These are the most common tasks and responsibilities that employers seek to outsource:

- eligibility determinations
- fulfillment of enrollment material
- preparation and distribution of notices and disclosures
- hardship determinations and loan approvals

- distribution requests
- vesting determinations
- employer contribution calculations

Recently, a new service offering has emerged from firms that offer to act as the 3(16) plan administrator under your single employer plan. In such an outsourcing arrangement, the vendor performs and is responsible for making ERISA determinations. However, some might argue that the 3(16) cannot be fully outsourced and that the offering creates something like a reiteration error. As we noted with the 3(38) investment manager, the plan sponsor still cannot abdicate its fiduciary status. The 3(16) plan administrator is still responsible for monitoring vendors and ensuring accurate and timely payroll functions, which revert back to employer control. Our observation is that the 3(16) outsourcing has been oversold, and we suggest instead that the plan sponsor delegate the common tasks we identified above while understanding that the employer retains the final responsibility as the plan administrator.

An Option to Enhance Your Corporate Liability Coverage

As distinct from the fiduciary warranty offered by a conflicted party-in-interest, a plan sponsor may purchase a fiduciary insurance policy from a property and casualty insurer. These policies may be included as part of a company's liability insurance package, along with board of directors' errors and omissions coverage. These policies may cover all ERISA benefits, retirement and medical, and protect the personal assets of fiduciaries from legal claims that the fiduciary breached their responsibilities. A fiduciary liability policy may be helpful where the 401(k) or 403(b) committee members or board members are otherwise reticent about serving in the fiduciary role. *Many plan sponsors believe incorrectly that the ERISA/fidelity bond required by DOL regulations is also protection for the fiduciary. The fidelity bond required by ERISA reimburses the plan in the event of employee theft of assets from the plan.*

A Corporate Trustee Adds Fiduciary Protection

The plan document and the Form 5500 identify the plan trustee. If you are receiving regular prospecting calls about your 401(k), there is a good chance you are listed as the signer of the 5500 or listed as an individual trustee. We recommend that plan sponsor fiduciaries replace themselves as individual trustee with the corporate trustee, also referred to as a directed trustee. The custodian/trustee of your plan, as we identified in chapter 1, is usually the same entity that can be assigned as the corporate trustee. This adds value to the plan in several ways that are not immediately obvious to the plan sponsor. There is often no additional cost for the corporate trustee.

When the handling and distribution of assets are controlled by a corporate trustee, plan participants receive an extra degree of protection that plan assets will be used solely to pay benefits to participants and beneficiaries, and approved plan expenses. The corporate trustee should only make distributions that are approved and allowed by the terms of the plan document. Moreover, the corporate trustee produces and certifies the financial statements for the plan. Plans with over one hundred participants subject to the plan audit requirement may pay a lower audit fee for a corporate trusteed plan, because the plan may be eligible to file a limited-scope audit report. The corporate trustee also prepares standardized auditor's reports designed to simplify the audit process.

Action Items

- ✓ Identify the internal and external plan fiduciaries for both investment and administrative requirements under ERISA.
- ✓ Establish a fiduciary governance process and document procedures and actions in a fiduciary file.

- ✓ Assure that all required ERISA tasks have been assigned or delegated to staff, vendors, or cofiduciaries.
- ✓ Minimize fiduciary risk by establishing and monitoring the three layers of defense: 404(c), QDIA, and an investment policy statement.

Chapter 4
Optimal Plan Design Strategies

P lan sponsors know they want and need to have a 401(k) plan because it is a necessary part of any employee benefit package. Employees expect to find a 401(k), and they ask about it during employment interviews (even if many do not enroll after asking). When we first sit down with prospective plan sponsor clients, they have a general expectation for the plan goals—provide a vehicle to help employees prepare for retirement, or perhaps to offer tax savings to the owners and managers. What we hear from employers most often is that they want to offer a plan that, in their terms, is "fair" and "reasonable."

Employers ask us for benchmarking specific to their industry or competitors. If your business is recruiting skilled employees in a competitive market, you should learn about the plan features that are competitive with your industry peers. What are the common eligibility, vesting, and contribution features? How often and what methods are used for enrollment? What are the loan and distribution options? What is the most common type of default investment, and how many and what type of funds are available in the investment menu?

The Form 5500 schedules collected by the Department of Labor are available at the DOL website and contain some plan design data points, but it has not been compiled in a format that is useful for broad comparisons. By downloading the DOL data, private firms (such as Fiduciary Benchmarks, Inc. and Judy Diamond) have created specialized databases and reports that can provide industry and plan comparisons among similar employers. *Plan Sponsor* magazine and the Profit Sharing Council of America sponsor surveys and produce benchmarking reports. Consulting firms and providers with a large number of plans have compiled data from their client populations. Vanguard publishes its annual "How America Saves" report with over one hundred data points on plan provisions and features covering eligibility, entry dates, contributions, distribution rules, investment options, and participant statistics.

You can tailor plan provisions to meet the specific needs and goals for your business. The optimal plan design reflects the best fit and a compromise among competing objectives for participation and benefit outcomes, ease of administration, and employer cost. We find two basic approaches to plan design.

Employee Benefit Approach to Plan Design

The employee benefit approach has the primary goal of providing a plan that will best prepare the majority of employees for retirement. The focus here is to limit as far as possible the roadblocks to participation and to encourage and enable employees to join the plan and participate in a way that will generate a secure and comfortable retirement. To achieve that goal, employees will need to reach a combined employee/employer contribution rate in the range of 10 percent to 15 percent of pay.

In our plan design work, we rely heavily on the surveys and findings from the field of behavioral finance as applied to employee behavior vis-à-vis retirement programs. In his book *Save More Tomorrow*, behavioral economist Professor Shlomo Benartzi provides solutions to the behavioral challenges that thwart employee retirement planning: inertia, limited self-control, loss aversion, and myopia. *Those who do not enroll when first provided the opportunity usually will not enroll at all.* The employee benefit approach to plan design steers employee participation and combines ease of use and automation with personalized communication and education programs.

Owner-Centric and Advanced Plan Design

The owner-centric plan design is popular with smaller firms, family businesses, and professional practices. Here, the objective is to provide an attractive plan to all employees, while also customizing plan provisions that provide cost-effective tax benefits to the favored participant group—owners, principals, and highly compensated managers. The owner-centric plan will provide a significant benefit to all participants, usually through a generous safe harbor contribution formula, but seeks to focus 80 percent or more of the employer contribution to the favored participant group. As we once reminded an IRS agent, although the owners might be receiving most of the contribution, they are paying 100 percent of the cost.

All 401(k) plan documents can allow for profit-sharing contributions. These across-the-board employer contributions do not require an employee contribution. Common provisions to skew benefits for highly compensated employees are the new comparability and the Social Security integrated profit-sharing methods. New comparability calculates larger contributions for older and more highly paid owners/managers by looking at the actuarial present value of benefits at retirement age, so that a small contribution to a younger employee has the equivalent value of a much larger contribution to an employee closer to age sixty-five.

Social Security integration allows a two-tiered compensation formula to determine an employer-funded profit-sharing contribution. The typical breakpoint is the Social Security taxable wage maximum ($127,200 in 2017). For example, compensation up to the breakpoint receives a 5 percent contribution, and compensation over the breakpoint receives a 10 percent contribution. Social Security integration is a permissible method of discrimination, based on the fact that the compensation cap on social security taxes is well above the commensurate maximum benefit for highly compensated employees. The Social Security retirement benefits formula skews heavily away from the highly compensated and toward the median wage earner. Thus, the IRS allows employers more leeway to make up the retirement benefits for highly compensated employees.

Employee Demographic Considerations

Plan sponsors should consider workforce characteristics such as average job tenure and turnover, education levels, and compensation ranges. These will all impact the cost of employer contributions and plan operations. Industry survey data provide some indication as how employees will respond to eligibility and entry date requirements, and to various matching formulas. Plan benefit studies can project matching contribution costs and possible results of discrimination testing.

A plan with many small account balances will have lower employer contribution costs but higher administrative costs as a percentage of plan assets. If the administrative costs are charged to plan assets as a percentage of plan assets, participants who have accumulated a large account balance or contribute the maximum contribution may perceive the plan less favorably.

The trend in the last decade is eligibility that is more liberal and entry dates on an immediate, monthly, or quarterly basis. Early and automatic participation eliminates one of the roadblocks to employee participation, as employees form the early habit of saving and adjust their spending and budgets accordingly. Most plans allow hardship withdrawal and loan provisions so that employees feel they can participate in the plan but also provide for emergencies. A stated, definitive employer match paid on the same frequency as employee deferrals is a highly visible benefit and provides positive reinforcement.

What if the plan has been offered to employees at a particular geographic location or to an employee classification in which very few or no employees have joined the plan voluntarily? This might be a case for an automatic enrollment program. Alternatively, the plan sponsor might consider a class exclusion referred to as a "carve-out," which we discuss later in this chapter.

Plan Cost and Administrative Considerations

For most companies, quarterly entry dates during the plan year are an attractive benefit provision for participants and provide the easiest and most compliance-friendly administration. Eligible employees must receive the various notices and plan material, and recordkeepers need employee census and address data to keep their systems current and prepare customized communications. During our plan design consultations with the plan sponsor, we assist in evaluating their internal capabilities to offer quarterly, monthly, or immediate enrollment dates.

Hardship withdrawals aid employee emergencies but require strict scrutiny according to DOL regulations. Loan features require payroll deduction repayment and may involve the plan sponsor in defaults and deemed distributions. Improper handling of these events can and does lead to employer penalties. There is a divergent consideration in regard to loan and withdrawal provisions to the extent they diminish plan assets. As aggregate plan assets increase, the plan enjoys greater economy of scale and has access to better provider services and plan features. On the other hand, employees may have immediate financial needs or desire access to their money.

Employers have overcome their initial concern that the Roth 401(k) feature would prove to be confusing to employees who already have choices and decisions to make about the plan options. In our experience, the Roth 401(k) has not been confusing to employees, because many are familiar with the concept through a Roth IRA, and besides, explaining a future pot of tax-exempt money is not a difficult task. Opening up the Roth 401(k) feature as an additional financial planning tool has been attractive for employees. The capabilities of the payroll provider must be determined before offering this feature.

In our earlier chapter 2, "Components of Every 401(k)," we mentioned the availability of both IRS-approved prototype and flexible customized documents. Here, we discuss plan provisions that are available within the economical prototype plan document used by most plan sponsors.

The Dreaded Refund

For some HR managers, every plan year brings confused, perplexed, and irate participants to their office in response to the dreaded refund. After the end of the plan year, the TPA or recordkeeper has determined that the plan has failed the average deferral percentage (ADP) or the average contribution percentage (ACP) tests. As a result, highly compensated employees (owners, family members, and employees earning over $120,000) receive a return of their contributions and earning thereon for amounts in excess of the permitted test result. Thus, an employee who contributed 10 percent of their pay may get a taxable refund that could lower their contribution to 4 percent of pay.

We feel your pain. You attended our education workshop, joined the plan, registered on the website to set goals and select investments, and monitored your progress. The government, employers, advisors, and the newspapers tell you to save for retirement, and then you get your money back!

If you are a participant in a plan subject to post-year testing, our advice is to maintain your desired contribution rate and do not adjust or try to anticipate the test results. It is better to overcontribute and receive a refund. The money will be taxable in the year received.

By the way, as the plan administrator, you should not *instruct* employees to not contribute an amount that is otherwise allowed by the plan document, even though you assume or know that a refund will be required. This is violation of ERISA and the plan document. As a convenience, you could *inform* the affected participants of likely test results.

As a plan administrator, you might consider an amendment to your plan document to use the prior year testing method. When calculated using the prior year method, the discrimination test uses the census and contribution data for the prior year, and the result is applied to the year going forward. In this way, all highly compensated participants are advised at the beginning of the year of their maximum contribution rate.

Safe Harbor Contribution Formulas

If your business includes owners, managers, highly compensated employees and their family members who wish to participate and benefit from the plan, the IRS discrimination and top-heavy tests may severely restrict their participation. It is both a disappointment and a nuisance for those key employees and owners to receive a taxable refund of their contributions. Operational failures can lead to IRS penalties and even disqualify plan assets from tax deferral. You should consult with a plan advisor or qualified plan specialist who can suggest and provide cost estimates for various safe harbor plan designs.

Two of the safe harbor contribution formulas are well known. In the first, the employer can offer a matching contribution, 100 percent vested, equal to 100 percent of the employee's first 3 percent of salary contribution and 50 percent of the next 2 percent of salary contribution. In effect, the employee contributes 5 percent of their pay and receives a 4 percent employer matching contribution. In the second version, the employer can provide to all eligible employees (defined as those who have reached age twenty-one and completed one year of service) an across-the-board 3 percent of compensation employer contribution. The employees do not need to make their own contribution as a condition for the 3 percent employer contribution.

Using either safe harbor formula, the plan satisfies discrimination and top-heavy requirements, so the owners and highly compensated employees (those earning more than $120,000 per year) may contribute their own personal maximum contribution and receive the employer contribution.

A third safe harbor contribution formula is referred to as the qualified automatic contribution arrangement (QACA) safe harbor. It is less well known since it became available more recently in connection with automatic enrollment, which we discuss below. Under the QACA safe harbor, the plan may use a two-year, 100 percent cliff vesting schedule and provides a match of 100 percent of the first 1 percent of employee contribution, and 50 percent match on the next 5 percent of employee salary contribution. Thus, an employee contributes 6 percent of pay and receives an employer match of 3.5 percent.

To use the QACA safe harbor, the plan must use the IRS procedures for automatic contribution, which provides initial employee automatic enrollment at 3 percent of pay, which would cost the employer a 2 percent matching contribution.

Automatic Enrollment: Serve the Plan on a Silver Platter

We have all been to a crowded cocktail party with friends and associates. Those delicious and expensive appetizers may go uneaten unless a server comes by to offer them to guests, and when the silver platter comes around, the delicacies disappear quickly. Think of automatic enrollment as a way you can offer the plan to employees on a silver platter.

Over the last several years, automatic enrollment has gained popularity with plan sponsors as a method to increase employee participation and ensure that no employee (or later beneficiary) can ever claim they were not offered the opportunity to join the plan. Higher participation will also improve the ADP/ACP discrimination test results.

A 2014 study by Vanguard of 1,400 small and midsize plans (most plans under $20 million in assets) found that plans with automatic enrollment have an overall participation rate of 87 percent, compared with a participation rate of only 62 percent for plans with voluntary enrollment. A study by Fidelity of 20,500 corporate DC plans and 11.5M participants as of 12/31/13 found that a little over 90 percent of automatically enrolled participants continued or increased their deferral rates. In the same study, auto-enrolled participants had average deferral rate of 4.9 percent.

Another 2014 study of Bank of America Merrill Lynch plans with automatic enrollment points to 32 percent higher average participation rates than plans that do not have automatic enrollment. The participation rate was 89 percent for employees automatically enrolled with a default contribution rate of 4 percent or less, and went to a higher 93 percent for employees with a default contribution rate of 5 percent or greater. At a default savings rate of 4 percent contribution, the employee opt-out rate of attrition was 11 percent. The opt-out rate declined to 5 percent for employees who were automatically enrolled at a 5 percent savings rate.

Think Automated, Not Mandatory Enrollment

Automatic enrollment is not and should not be confused with mandatory enrollment. This misunderstanding convinced many employers to forego this provision. Think of the term *automated enrollment*. Eligible employees are notified of the automatic enrollment procedures and have an opportunity to elect a different contribution percentage, or to elect a zero contribution percentage. Only those employees who have made no election, in other words, did not respond at all to the invitation to enroll, will be automatically enrolled in the plan at the default deferral amount.

For plans that intend to use the QACA safe harbor regulations regarding automatic enrollment, the automatic contributions cannot exceed 10 percent and must be at least 3 percent during the initial plan year, increasing to 4 percent during the second plan year, increasing to 5 percent during the third plan year, and increasing to 6 percent during any subsequent plan years.

The typical automatic enrollment percentage is 3 percent, which we consider inadequate. The 3 percent is an unfortunate accident of history. When the Department of Labor issued automatic enrollment regulations, it used 3 percent as an example, and so 3 percent was widely copied into plan documents. However, do the math and consider that 3 percent for an employee at $50,000 salary is contributing $1,500, which in thirty years might amount to $100,000, or about one-quarter of a meaningful retirement benefit.

Both our experience and behavioral finance research show that over time, the employee enrolled at 3 percent is slightly more likely to drop out of the program than the employee enrolled automatically at 5 percent. Some of the 3 percent enrollees look at their paycheck and account statement and convince themselves that progress is hopeless. Auto-enrolled employees can stop their contribution at any time, but, depending on the plan population under study, some 80 percent to 90 percent of employees who are enrolled automatically will remain plan participants.

The Downside of Automatic Enrollment

When the employer has a fixed dollar budget for employer matching contributions, the addition of automatically enrolled participants and automatic increases will increase employer matching contribution costs. This might result in a lower rate of match for the participants who enrolled voluntarily. Also, the newly enrolled participant accounts have a higher cost to account balance ratio. Depending on the pricing formula for plan administration and how expenses are allocated, the long-term participants might experience or notice an increase in plan costs. This could be alleviated by using a per capita recordkeeping cost structure where each participant pays an equal quarterly fee. The surveys of automatic enrollment plans show that the participants who are defaulted into the plan at a low rate of 3 percent will tend to remain at that low level, whereas employees who voluntarily enroll are likely to select a higher rate of contribution.

Use Automatic Escalation for Gradual Improvement

Keep in mind the behavioral law of inertia. Those employees enrolled at 3 percent or 5 percent will remain at that rate. The solution to this problem is automatic escalation, which is the companion to automatic enrollment. Automatic escalation increases the employee's contribution rate by 1 percent each year until they reach the cap set by the plan, or as much as 10 percent. Fidelity Investments reviewed the automatic escalation results for 20,500 corporate retirement plans with 11.5 million participants as of 12/31/13. Their study showed that automatic escalation accounts for 36 percent of all deferral rate increases. In other words, one out of three employees increased their savings rate because it was automatic. Among the age twenty to twenty-four cohort, the effects are magnified: 63 percent of younger participants increased deferral rates due to automatic escalation.

As employers see the shortcomings of automatic enrollment as a standalone provision, they are overcoming their initial hesitancy to automatic increases, and we now see more adoption of this provision.

Stretch the Match

Almost all our clients, when they established their plan, asked a simple question with regard to the matching contribution: what do most plans do? The most common nonsafe harbor plan has a 50 percent match on a 6 percent of compensation employee contribution for a combined savings rate of 9 percent. The problem with this approach is that, unlike Garrison Keiler's Lake Wobegan where all the children are above average, the average 401(k) plan is not doing as well as it could.

As set forth in the book *Save More Tomorrow* by Professor Shlomo Benartzi, employees perceive and act on the cap of the match, more so than the matching rate. In other words, participants will tend to contribute up to the maximum cap on the match. If the employer sets the match at 40 percent of 8 percent (in place of 50 percent of 6 percent), a high percentage of the participants will "stretch" their contribution to 8 percent, and their combined employee and employer savings rate will increase to 11.2 percent of compensation. In this combination, there would be a slight increase of employer cost as employees respond to the incentive. The higher average deferral rate will also improve discrimination test results.

For another example, if your plan matches 100 percent with a cap of 3 percent, you can stretch the cap on the match to 6 percent with a 50 percent match. Employees will increase their contribution to 6 percent at no additional cost to the company.

Perhaps an employer wants to start auto-enrollment but is concerned matching costs will spike if participation rises from 70 percent to 90 percent. Given the behavioral assumptions, we can stretch the match to increase participation at very little increase in the employer's cost. The table below illustrates the likely cost scenarios of a typical matching plan with a 50 percent employer match up to 6 percent employee deferral enhanced with a stretch match and automatic enrollment. The first row represents the status quo of voluntary enrollment and 70 percent payroll participation; the Options 1, 2, and 3 rows below assume that payroll participation has increased to 90 percent through automatic enrollment.

	The Formula	Likely Employee Deferral	Combined Employee/Employer Deferral	Employer Cost (% of Payroll)
Status Quo	50¢ up to 6%	6.0%	9.0%	2.10%
Option 1	25¢ up to 6%	6.0%	7.5%	1.35%
Option 2	20¢ up to 10%	10.0%	12.0%	1.80%
Option 3	25¢ up to 10%	10.0%	12.5%	2.25%

Source: "Save for Tomorrow: Practical Behavioral Finance Solutions To Improve 401(k) Plans" by Shlomo Benartzi with Roger Lewin, 2012

You will notice that Options 1, 2, and 3 would each cause an employer benefit cutback in terms of the match received from the employer. With automatic enrollment, more employees would be participating at a lower employer match rate. To avoid a reduced matching contribution, the employer would need to increase the matching formula to $0.30 up to 10 percent, and aggregate payroll contribution costs would increase to 2.7 percent. (Note: within the language and discrimination testing parameters of a typical prototype document, it is unlikely that the plan can provide for separate matching formulas for existing and newly hired employees. Also, these stretch match examples do not meet matching safe harbor guidelines.)

An Ideal Plan

If a plan sponsor wanted to start the design process with the ideal plan provisions from the standpoint of participant outcomes, we would recommend these provisions:

- automatic enrollment and re-enrollment at 5 percent to 6 percent
- automatic escalation at 1 percent to 2 percent / year (preferably in conjunction with annual compensation adjustments) up to 12 percent

- stretch match of 25 percent to 40 percent
- QDIA: target date funds or risk portfolio model
- no hardship withdrawals; allow for one plan loan at a time
- twenty-first-century loan provisions (electronic bill paying, allowing continuation of loan payments after separation, and even loan initiation after separation)
- best practices fee structure—per capita administrative fee each quarter, transaction fees for voluntary withdrawals, loans, and QDROs (where participant fees cover almost all plan expenses)
- Roth and pretax deferrals available
- accept rollovers while employed and after separation (including Roth, tax-deductible, and after-tax IRAs)

Class Exclusions

Some businesses have groups of employees at a location or in job classifications that will rarely if ever join the plan. They may have a short-term or temporary attachment to the company. Perhaps they are working entry-level positions at minimum wage and expect to terminate employment or progress to a more permanent career type of employment with the company. Nevertheless, if the company has immediate or early eligibility and enrollment dates, they will become eligible for the plan. These eligible employees are required to receive all the plan enrollment and educational material as well as all the notices and disclosures. Furthermore, when the number of employees in the total eligible population is over one hundred in a new plan (or increases over the trigger point of 120 employees in an existing plan), the plan sponsor will be required to engage a qualified plan accountant to audit the plan every year. Moreover, if these employees do not join the plan, it is likely the plan will fail discrimination tests and prohibit the highly compensated employees from any useful participation in the plan.

Under IRS-permissible class exclusions, an employer may define a group of employees for exclusion from participation as long as the plan can meet minimum coverage rules. Subject to the IRS coverage tests, the plan can exclude an entire location or class of employees from the plan. Any employee within the excluded class as defined in the plan document will not be eligible to participate in the plan, until or unless they become employed in a covered class.

Although the IRS approves this provision in a prototype plan, not all product or service providers will offer this exclusion.

Maximizing Benefits for High-Income Participants

Cash balance plans are a type of defined benefit plan that offer the maximum qualified plan tax shelter available under the IRS code. A highly compensated owner at age fifty and earning at or over the annual plan compensation limit ($270,000 in 2017) may be able to receive a tax-deductible contribution as high as $133,000 for their own plan account, in addition to the $53,000 maximum they could contribute to their 401(k) plan with a new comparability profit-sharing feature. Moreover, an additional $6,000 for the age fifty catch-up brings the grand annual total to $192,000. The cash balance contribution maximum climbs higher with each year closer to retirement age sixty-five, so, for example, a sixty-year-old owner or partner may receive a $228,000 cash balance contribution for a grand annual total annual of $287,000, which includes the companion 401(k) profit-sharing plan.

In order to satisfy various IRS coverage and discrimination rules, the cash balance plan is usually paired with a safe harbor 401(k) profit-sharing plan. The general design approach considers the demographic composition of the group—older, highly compensated owners and younger, lower-paid employees provides the most advantage to the owner. Cash balance and defined benefit plans skew much higher benefits toward age, long tenure, and high compensation. The 401(k) plan is utilized to provide most of the benefit to employees. This is a cost-effective way to provide the minimum benefit requirements to the non-highly-compensated employees and pass the required tests for coverage. While the owner or partner group will receive the maximum benefit allowed by law, the employees fare well, too, and may receive a 7 percent to 10 percent contribution.

Where qualified plan designs cannot satisfy discrimination tests, corporate entities sometimes use nonqualified deferred compensation plans to provide a savings program for highly compensated employees. Nonqualified plans are not available under IRS prototype rules, involve a substantial risk of forfeiture by the employee, and require the assistance of a tax attorney or tax advisor to prepare the document.

Action Items

- ✓ Determine which approach is suitable or preferred for your plan design—employee benefit or owner-centric approach. What are the goals and objectives of the plan?
- ✓ Consult benchmark and survey resources for comparisons with similar plans in your industry.
- ✓ Avoid discrimination test failures and contribution refunds by safe harbor and/or automatic enrollment plan design.
- ✓ To increase employee contribution rates, stretch the matching formula to maximize employee rate of contribution.

Chapter 5

"My Plan Is Free" and Secrets of Plan Pricing

There is no such thing as a free lunch.
—Milton Friedman,
Nobel Prize–winning economist

As a plan fiduciary, think of yourself as the CFO of the plan and watch costs as you would any other aspect of your business. If your health insurance rate doubles, you will notice immediately and painfully. However, with retirement plans, the costs can run out of control without being detected, and participants will bear the consequences. You must determine that fees are "reasonable" and pay attention to how they are allocated. Some plan sponsors elect to have the company pay the recordkeeping and administrative expenses, as a generous and attractive benefit to participants. These costs are an additional tax-deductible expense for the company. However, as you will see in this chapter, it is possible and even likely that the recordkeeping fees (including TPA) and plan advisory fees have been shifted and hidden within the investment fees component.

The general rule and presumption under ERISA is that assets

are held in trust for the exclusive benefit of participants and that no expenses can be paid to a fiduciary or any party-in-interest. Such payments are a "prohibited transaction" under ERISA, unless they are specifically permitted by the Department of Labor through "prohibited transaction exemptions." Over decades, the DOL has issued exemptions and advisory opinions on the general rule. ERISA Section 408(b)(2) allows for payment by a plan to a party-in-interest if no more than reasonable compensation is paid for such service. The Department of Labor has stated the guiding principle for plan sponsors as to plan services: "Among other duties, fiduciaries have a responsibility to ensure that the services provided to their plan are necessary and that the cost of those services is reasonable."

Concerned that a lack of fee transparency hindered efforts by all parties to compare and manage plan costs, the Department of Labor issued fee disclosure regulations in 2012 (under Sections 408(b)(2) and 404(a)(5) of ERISA). Taken together, they require covered plan vendors and service providers to disclose their fees to plan sponsors, who in turn must disclose plan costs to participants on a regular basis in a standard format. Plan sponsors must also evaluate the fees to determine whether they are "reasonable" in relation to the services provided. For plans generally exceeding one hundred participant account balances, the DOL also revised the annual Form 5500 Schedule C to include additional fee and expense data from all entities receiving direct compensation from the plan and indirect compensation (e.g., revenue sharing) in excess of $5,000 for services rendered to the plan, as well as fiduciaries and certain service providers receiving compensation in excess of $1,000 from sources besides the plan.

In the decades before fee disclosure, it was common for plan sponsors with some of the most overpriced plans to say "my plan is free," because the many layers of plan expenses were hidden, or, if you want to use the more neutral terms, embedded or implicit. To let employers and the retirement industry understand how serious the DOL considers the issue, it published a booklet called *A Look at 401(k) Fees* and included the following explanation:

> Assume that you are an employee with 35 years until retirement and a current 401(k) account balance of $25,000.

If returns on investments in your account over the next 35 years average 7 percent and fees and expenses reduce your average returns by 0.5 percent, your account balance will grow to $227,000 at retirement, even if there are no further contributions to your account.

If fees and expenses are 1.5 percent, however, your account balance will grow to only $163,000.

The 1 percent difference in fees and expenses would reduce your account balance at retirement by 28 percent.

Plan Sponsor and Participant Fee Disclosures

In order for plan sponsors to make informed decisions, with "apples to apples" comparisons, the ERISA 408(b)(2) regulations require plan service providers to disclose detailed information about their compensation and services. Your plan service providers must provide you a fee disclosure document at least annually and whenever there is a change in fees. This is referred to as a 408(b)(2) disclosure. The DOL has suggested and industry providers have adopted a standard format and charts to disclose and define fees. Under the companion regulation to ERISA 404(a)(5), the plan sponsor must then distribute fee disclosure information to the participants. If a plan sponsor utilizes revenue sharing from plan assets to pay all or a portion of the plan's administrative expenses, the quarterly disclosures must include a statement to this effect.

There are no DOL penalties stipulated for failure to provide these disclosures. However, perhaps worse, failure to comply with the participant disclosure requirements is a breach of fiduciary duty and exposes the plan sponsor to participant lawsuits or suit by the DOL. Additionally, the plan loses the Section 404(c) fiduciary protection that we said earlier is a cornerstone of protection.

Below, we look in more detail at the cost elements of a plan, both direct and indirect. A direct expense, such as a monthly participant account charge, is deducted directly from plan assets or billed to the plan sponsor. These are easily discoverable by the plan sponsor. Asset-based fees, per-participant fees, transaction-based fees, and flat fees are forms of direct compensation to the vendor. Fees such as loan initiation and servicing fees, withdrawal and distribution fees, and fees for utilization of advice or managed account services are typically borne by the plan participants and show up as a deduction on the participant's quarterly statement. The plan sponsor has a fiduciary responsibility to determine that these fees are reasonable for the service provided.

Indirect costs may be built into the investment account or mutual fund and facilitate payment to one or more of the plan providers—broker, investment manager, recordkeeper, custodian, or trust company. Investment management, 12b-1 distribution fees, and Sub-Transfer Agency (Sub-TA fees) incurred inside mutual funds are indirect expenses. The types of indirect and direct expenses will vary according to the providers involved in your plan. From the fee disclosures given to you by the providers, you will be able to identify which of these provider compensation expenses apply to your plan.

The term "revenue sharing" refers to money paid by a fund company (investment manager) or insurance company to a custodian, brokerage firm, TPA, or recordkeeper in return for services provided. The rate of revenue sharing, if any, is negotiated by and between the various components of your plan and may differ between plans and parties. The mutual fund paying a higher revenue sharing rate to the custodian, broker-dealer, or recordkeeper may have preferential placement within the 401(k) product offered to your company. Or, you may be told that a fund with lower or zero revenue sharing may not be available in your 401(k) plan.

Party-in-Interest: Value Add, Benign Influence, or Conflict of Interest?

Plans are sold through many different distribution channels and, accordingly, priced in a variety of ways, so comparisons can be difficult. Despite all the pages of disclosure, there is one important and obvious element that is not considered carefully enough: parties-in-interest. Take, for instance, the situation where the recordkeeper is also one of the investment fund managers, or the investment fund manager also serves as the plan advisor. Your company's banking relationship manager may introduce you to their 401(k) department, or your health insurance agent's broker also offers 401(k) products. Your payroll company maintains data on employee compensation and offers to facilitate 401(k) remittances. These might be beneficial value-add arrangements, benign influences, or real conflicts of interest. An example of the latter would be a situation where an investment option is included in the plan because of payments or favorite partner arrangements with the recordkeeper. You will need to uncover them and make a determination that the arrangement is in the overall best interests of the plan.

When the recordkeeper or custodian also offers its own funds in the plan investment menu, there is a tendency for poorly performing proprietary funds to remain in the plan while other outside, nonproprietary funds are more frequently replaced for poor performance. The relationship managers at the provider may have an incentive to keep assets in their own funds, or they may be more familiar with their own funds and unable to provide in-depth analysis of outside funds. The pricing of your plan may be conditioned on assets invested in proprietary funds. We have observed this bias, and in 2015, a trio of researchers from the Federal Reserve System, Indiana University, and the University of Texas confirmed the proprietary effect. In their findings, plans removed 13.7 percent of proprietary funds performing in the lowest 10 percent of their class, compared to 25.5 percent removal for nonproprietary, external funds not favored by the recordkeeper (Veronika Krepely Pool, Clemens Sialm, and Irina Stefanescu, "It Pays to Set the Menu: Mutual Fund Investment Options in 401(k) Plans," *Journal of Finance* [August 14, 2015], available at SSRN: http://ssrn.com/abstract=2112263 or http://dx.doi.org/10.2139/ ssrn.2112263).

Recordkeeping fees are one of the major components of plan cost and sometimes are more difficult to isolate because they may be applied in different ways. Recordkeeping services (whether from an insurance company, mutual fund, bank, or direct platform recordkeeper) may be charged based on a percentage of plan assets (for example, twenty basis points, which is equal to .20 percent of assets), a flat dollar amount per participant (for example, $100 per account balance), or a combination of both.

Insurance company products using a group annuity contract handle recordkeeping and custodial services and combine those with an array of investments options. The group annuity contract may offer a combination of public mutual funds, collective trusts, and separate account investments, and each could have a different structure for expenses. Terms like wrap fee, contract charge, asset charge, separate account charge, and administration fee indicate sources of recordkeeper or product provider revenue, and they may be explicitly deducted from participant accounts, hidden, or a combination of both. In addition to 12b-1 and Sub-TA sources of revenue derived from internal mutual funds, group annuity contracts may have revenue sharing through contract and asset charges that are "wrapped" around the investments. Miscellaneous fees may be debited directly from accounts or billed to the plan sponsor as a charge to plan participants for account maintenance, investment exchanges, loans, and distributions.

The 408(b) (2) fee disclosure will list the types and sources of compensation to the recordkeeper. Here is where the plan sponsor may lose the trail of costs. The recordkeeper's compensation may be paid by any one or more of these methods:

- a direct invoice to the employer
- an explicit deduction from plan assets shown on the aggregate plan statement and participant statements
- hidden revenue paid to the recordkeeper from one or more of the investment options

Sources of hidden revenue can be very difficult to detect. Recordkeeping fees may be lowered, offset, or subsidized based on the amount of assets that participants direct to an insurance company general account or fixed interest account. The real cost to the plan and a participant is the lower interest rate received on the proprietary interest account, compared to the rate paid in a lower cost share class or in a market competitive product. A similar cost is incurred when recordkeeping fees are lowered or waived based on the inclusion or utilization of certain investment options favored by the recordkeeper.

Third-party administrator (TPA) fees will be incurred when plan services are unbundled and the recordkeeper is not providing the plan document and compliance/administration elements of the plan. The TPA's service agreement and fee disclosure will show the fees, which are paid mostly by direct invoice to the plan sponsor.

TPAs usually charge a fixed fee based on the number of eligible employees or the number of participants. The definition of "participant" is a common misunderstanding and an important consideration for employers with a high number of eligible employees and low participation. Participants might be defined as any eligible employees, whether they are enrolled or not, plus terminated participants with account balances. Recordkeepers tend to charge based on the number of account balances—that is, the number of individuals for whom they have accounts with a balance.

TPAs may also collect a variable fee based on the value of plan assets, which may be hidden in the form of revenue sharing, subsidies, and sales bonuses. The TPA is not "free." If they are paid by the plan recordkeeper, the cost is embedded in the recordkeeper's product and therefore paid by participants. Some TPAs are scrupulous in deducting this revenue from their invoice to the plan sponsor, but others retain the revenue as additional income to the TPA. Regardless of the sources or types of compensation to the TPA, your responsibility is to determine the real cost and judge the value of services.

Trust/custodian costs are an element and cost of plan operations. This cost is a line item that is off the radar screen, usually embedded in the recordkeeping operation. If the plan is "unbundled" to the extent that the custodian is a separate entity from the recordkeeper or investment funds, then the plan will be charged explicitly for these fees, usually in the range of three to five basis points (or .03 to .05 percent of assets).

Plan advisory fees may be charged as a percentage of assets or, for larger plans, on a flat-dollar basis, or a combination of the two. Plan advisors, including insurance agents and registered representatives, are usually paid in one form or another from plan assets. A fiduciary plan advisor is usually paid an explicit fee charged against plan assets and reported on participant statements. Brokers and agents are usually paid from the plan provider (insurance company or mutual fund), which has embedded this cost in the investment funds or product contract.

Audit fees will apply for plans over one hundred participants that are required to attach an independent audit with the annual Form 5500 filing. Usually, we see the employer paying this cost. It is invoiced to the plan sponsor from the independent CPA firm, although it may be charged and paid out of plan assets. Attorney fees for drafting a plan document are invoiced to the plan sponsor and as "settlor expenses" are not eligible to be paid from plan assets.

The US Supreme Court Weighs In on Mutual Fund Expenses

In one of its less controversial and unanimous decisions, *Tibble et al. v. Edison International*, the Supreme Court found that a plan sponsor has a duty to continually monitor and remove imprudent investments and specifically pointed to mutual fund share class expenses. The participants claimed that they suffered high and unreasonable investment expenses as the plan assets grew over time. The plan sponsor, Edison International, breached its fiduciary duty of prudence by selecting retail share classes rather than institutional share classes of mutual funds in the 401(k) investment menu.

As we examine below the components of mutual fund expense, it is not hard to see how Edison International found itself in a fiduciary predicament. Mutual fund expenses are the easiest to access and uncover, but they are built into complicated structures and choices for plan sponsors to untangle.

In all public mutual funds, you will find one or more of the following three categories of mutual fund expenses, *all included in the total expense of the fund as shown in the prospectus*:

Investment management fees cover the cost of investing the fund assets and include transaction and operating expenses of the fund. This is the pure cost to you, the participant investor, of having your money invested and sharing in the portfolio. From index to active fund styles, the investment management fees may range from .05 percent to 1 percent or higher.

12b-1 fees are referred to as distribution expenses and are paid by the mutual fund from fund assets, including commissions to brokers, for marketing expenses and other administrative services. In a 401(k) plan, they are a source of *revenue sharing* and are charged as a percentage of the portfolio assets and deducted from the investment return. 12b-1 fees may range from .25 percent to 1.00 percent.

Sub-TA (transfer agency) fees are another source of *revenue sharing* and are paid as a percentage of assets and/or as a flat dollar amount per investor/participant. Sub-TA fees are paid to recordkeepers and fund administrators to compensate them for handling fund recordkeeping, custody, disclosure, and administrative services. The ostensible rationale is that in a 401(k) plan the recordkeeper issues statements and disclosures to the individual participants and the mutual fund company is spared the cost. These fees range from 0 percent to .50 percent, or a flat $12 to $20 per participant fund position.

Example of R1 to R6 Share Classes

Share Class	R1	R2	R3	R4	R5	R6
Manager Fee	0.35%	0.35%	0.35%	0.35%	0.35%	0.35%
12b-1 Fees	1.00%	0.75%	0.50%	0.25%	0.00%	0.00%
Sub-TA Fees	0.10%	0.25%	0.15%	0.10%	0.05%	0.00%
Total Fund Expense Ratio	1.45%	1.35%	1.00%	0.70%	0.40%	0.35%

The chart above dissects the fee structure of a mutual fund commonly used in 401(k) plans. The fund company may offer as many as six different share classes, each with its own ticker symbol. The chart illustrates the cost variations for six different share classes ranging from R1 to R6. Other firms may use different nomenclature for their share class variations. The key point here is that the same investment option (meaning the identical portfolio of investments and manager) can be purchased by the plan and offered to participants with zero, low, or high levels of revenue sharing for providers. The challenge for plan sponsors is to keep aware of the payment amounts, track the parties who are receiving them, and determine that the payments are "reasonable" for the services rendered in a competitive market and that those services are necessary.

Note the variation in 12b-1 and Sub-TA fees that are offered to accommodate vendor preferences for broker-dealer compensation and recordkeeping revenue, respectively. The R6 share class has zero revenue sharing, and the sole expense is the investment management fee. You should understand that without revenue sharing, the other service parties would need to recoup their charges from the plan assets or plan sponsor through other direct billing. So, for example, the recordkeeper may deduct its fee from the participant accounts or invoice the plan sponsor.

Here is a look at how the revenue sharing, if any, might be applied by three different recordkeepers and financial advisor/agent arrangements using various share classes:

Examples:

- Using R2 shares, Recordkeeping Firm #1 may not directly charge its client for services but receives 1.00 percent in combined 12b-1 and Sub-TA fees; an insurance company may use some of this money to pay the agent a finder's fee and trailing commission.
- Using R3 shares, Recordkeeping Firm #2 may directly charge its client $4,000 for recordkeeping services but actually earns a total of $5,000, including $1,000 from .15 percent of subtransfer agency fees. The broker-dealer of the financial advisor receives the .50 percent of 12b-1 fees.
- Using R4 shares, Recordkeeping Firm #3 may charge its client $4,000 for recordkeeping services and credit an ERISA account with the 12b-1 and Sub-TA revenue equal to a total .35 percent or $2,333. The plan sponsor uses the credit to pay the invoice of the fee-based plan advisor.

The Total Transparency Arrangement: Zero Revenue Sharing

From the standpoint of transparency and managing costs within the plan, at Everhart Advisors we seek out and prefer, if available, vendors and investment funds that can offer a pure investment management fee without revenue sharing. In the chart above, the R6 share class is lowest cost and has no revenue sharing. The zero-revenue fund may also be referred to as an "Institutional" or "I" share. The plan sponsor can then isolate recordkeeping, administration, and advisor costs and negotiate appropriate fee arrangements. Zero revenue sharing also has the advantage of enabling uniform expense treatment for all participants. Unfortunately, there are still excellent fund families that do not offer a zero-revenue share class for retirement plans. For some fund companies, your plan might need to exceed $100 million before you can access the zero revenue share class.

"Better Than Free"—Bookkeeping Accounts and ERISA Buckets

Some years ago, a curious CFO asked, "If my plan was free at $5 million in assets, how come it is not better than free at $10 million?" He had stumbled upon the revenue sharing paradox. As the plan assets grow, the plan should enjoy more economy of scale and therefore fees as a percentage of assets should be adjusted downward. The work involved for recordkeeping a plan with one hundred participants with $2 million of assets is not five times greater when the plan grows to $10 million with the same headcount.

Even before the DOL Fee Disclosure in 2012, plan sponsors were becoming aware of revenue sharing arrangements between mutual funds, broker-dealers, and recordkeepers and began to expect revenue sharing to come back to their plan. Recordkeepers responded by creating credit accounts to share revenue back to the plan. In the common practice, the recordkeeper captures the revenue supporting its cost and credits the excess to the plan into an unallocated credit account. The monies in this account cannot be returned to the plan sponsor company or used for employee contributions; however, they can be applied to plan expenses, including recordkeeping, audit, advisory, administration, compliance, and education, or allocated to participants in proportion to their account balance. Of course, keep in mind that the revenue sharing is $0 when the investment funds have no revenue sharing 12b-1 or Sub-TA expenses.

There are two common approaches used by recordkeepers to this sharing arrangement with plan sponsors. The "bookkeeping" approach is a debit entry / credit account on the balance sheet of the recordkeeper. It is an asset of the recordkeeper, and the credit is determined by a contractual formula devised by the recordkeeper. The amount credited in the bookkeeping bucket will not equal the revenue generated by the plan assets; the recordkeeper is first deducting its expenses and retaining a portion. The excess is available to the plan sponsor to utilize or allocate to participants. Some recordkeepers allow the credits in the account to rollover to the following plan year. If the plan sponsor terminates the relationship with the recordkeeper, the recordkeeping contract may provide that the credit amounts are forfeited in part or whole.

The other approach is the "ERISA account" where a separate unallocated account within the plan is set up to capture the revenue generated by the revenue-sharing mutual funds. A small fee equal to 5 percent of revenue recaptured may apply in order to pay for the collection and accounting process. The IRS generally requires that a plan sponsor expend any monies held an ERISA account by the end of the plan year in accordance with plan terms (e.g., allocated to participants or used to pay plan expenses). The revenue sharing account was a major industry development and step forward for better transparency and lower plan costs. However, upon closer examination, these accounts present some issues of equitable distribution.

Fee Leveling between Participants

As we noted above, not all mutual funds have a zero-revenue share class. So, the plan investment menu may include a mix of mutual funds with zero-revenue share classes with funds that pay various rates of revenue sharing. Consider a plan with several zero-revenue sharing funds. These funds have low, investment management only costs and no revenue sharing to support plan recordkeeping and other services. The same plan's investment menu also has funds with various rates of 12b-1 or Sub-TA fees, maybe ten, twenty-five, or fifty basis points. Let us say one participant selects all zero-revenue sharing funds and those funds generate no revenue. Another participant is using funds that generate fifty basis points of revenue. The revenue is deposited into an unallocated credit account from which the employer pays plan expenses. Or perhaps the credit account is allocated back to all participants. One employee is effectively subsidizing another. If the employee with zero-revenue sharing funds also happens to be an owner or senior manager with a large account balance, the rank-in-file are paying the costs.

Several recordkeepers now offer to allocate the revenue to the particular participant whose investment choices generated that revenue. This is called fee leveling. The participant account with zero-revenue share funds may be debited a charge for plan expenses; the participant account with ample revenue sharing may be credited for amounts in excess of the allocated plan expenses. The earliest recordkeeping solutions to handle this problem used an imperfect monthly or quarterly accounting of revenue from participant fund holdings. Monthly or quarterly revenue sharing adjustments might not accurately reflect the individual participant's investment exchanges, market fluctuations, and contributions. This opened up the risk that participants would discover a timing loophole and game the system by investment changes. More recently, recordkeepers have developed the technology to provide daily fee leveling. Fee leveling on a daily basis avoids the intra-plan recordkeeping issues among participants.

What Expenses Can Be Deducted from the Plan or Credit Account / ERISA Bucket?

Depending on the type of credit account or ERISA bucket, your recordkeeping provider will give you guidance on what items are permissible to charge against the account. This may differ according to the recordkeeping contract. We find that most recordkeepers with credit accounts / ERISA buckets will allow the revenue-sharing assets to pay for recordkeeping fees, plan advisory and education costs, TPA and administrative costs, mailing and notice fulfillment, and audit expenses. Expenses for a companion cash balance plan would not be eligible. Employer expenses related to establishing the plan, such as a custom document, are not allowed as a deduction from plan assets.

With the proper documentation and accounting, the costs of company employee time dedicated to plan administration may be paid from plan assets. You should consult with legal counsel for questions particular to your plan, as this is a complex legal issue referred to as "settlor" and "nonsettlor" expenses. The rules apply to expenses applied to plan assets. Settlor expenses include the cost of any services provided to establish, terminate, or design the plan. These are the types of services that generally are seen as benefiting the employer, rather than the plan beneficiaries. The plan sponsor must pay these directly. Administrative expenses include fees and costs associated with things like amending the plan to keep it in compliance with tax laws, conducting nondiscrimination testing, performing participant recordkeeping services, or providing plan information to participants. These nonsettlor expenses can be paid by the plan.

Payments to parties-in-interest are a prohibited transaction under ERISA. It only seems common that expenses are deducted, because over decades since ERISA passed, the Department of Labor has issued exemptions to the general rule, on the condition that expenses are deemed necessary and reasonable for the services provided.

Revenue Sharing—The Case for and Against

As noted above, revenue sharing refers to money that is collected from plan assets and paid to service providers—recordkeepers, custodians, TPAs, broker-dealers, and plan advisors. As a participant looking at the share class chart above, you would obviously choose the R6 share class—that is, the share class with the absolute lowest expense. The lowest share class for investment management is simple to disclose and easy to explain. It also avoids the need to track and justify the 12b-1 and Sub-TA revenue sharing payments retained by the parties-in-interest, which payments created the problem for the plan sponsor in the *Tibble vs. Edison International* case.

Even with revenue sharing recapture into credit accounts with year-end reallocation to the participant, consider that the participant's investment expenses are deducted daily, but the credit may be returned as much as one year later. On the other hand, the revenue sharing is a source to pay the service providers. Without the revenue sharing, either the company plan sponsor will pay the costs directly or the costs will be deducted explicitly from plan assets and therefore shown as a deduction on participant quarterly statements.

Many employers and industry providers fear that employees might not join the plan if they are aware of the expenses. The large majority of plans for decades have used revenue sharing, mostly unbeknownst to the plan sponsor, because the products and providers did not offer any other arrangement. The hidden revenue sharing is the arrangement that led employers to think, *My plan is free*. And, before the DOL fee disclosure rules, it was a simple way to present the plan to employees.

Think about your policy toward plan expenses and then document your decision in your investment and expense policy statement. Are expenses paid by the employer, or paid by the plan assets and participants? If the company's policy is to have the plan expenses paid by plan assets, then one could argue that the cost is the same—whether deducted from plan assets and shown openly as a deduction on participant statements, or "hidden" in the revenue sharing arrangements.

As the plan sponsor, you may have precluded any expense policy choice altogether when you selected your plan product or recordkeeper. Many products and providers do not offer the lowest cost share class without some kind of revenue sharing, wrap, or asset charge. However, this is changing rapidly. We prefer and encourage our plan sponsor clients to use the lowest cost share class whenever available, to minimize revenue sharing and to educate employees with full disclosure and transparency of expenses.

Pro Rata or Per Capita Pricing—Deciding How Participants Pay for Plan Services

With the recent popularity of transparent pricing and plan revenue sharing in ERISA buckets and credit accounts, more plan sponsors now have a choice between pro rata and per capita pricing for recordkeeping services. Pro rata pricing is based on a percentage of the plan assets or participant account balance. For example, assume an annual administration charge of .50 percent is being levied against plan assets with each participant paying directly or indirectly based on their account balance. All plans with wrap fees, 12b-1, or Sub-TA expenses are pro rata pricing, because the expense is based on a percentage of assets. The participant with the $100,000 account balance is paying $500 toward the plan administration items, such as the Form 5500 filing, quarterly statements, website, and so on. The participant with a $10,000 balance is paying only $50 toward these same plan overhead expenses. Terminated participants with small accounts are subsidized by the active participants. One could say that the loyal customer is being overcharged. The plan could become unattractive to the higher account balance participants, and they may seek to withdraw their funds as soon as allowable. Or, one could argue that the employee with the larger account balance receives a greater tax benefit from the plan, and the small expense for new participants is encouragement to join.

The other approach is per capita (per head) pricing with a flat quarterly fee for each participant. Think of this approach as an equal admission price for all to the 401(k) park. Long-term participants are rewarded with lower costs, and newer participants are encouraged to make best use of the 401(k) facility. The per capita fee may also be an incentive for terminated participants with small account balances to withdraw their accounts.

Three Principles for Managing Plan Costs

We follow three principles to manage plan costs. Firstly, calculate your recordkeeping and TPA costs in total on a per-participant flat dollar amount, which should fall in the typical range of $60 to $120 annually. Your vendors may charge on some other basis, and you may decide to allocate the cost to participants pro rata or per capita, but evaluate recordkeeping overhead on a fixed-dollar basis. The service and technology investment of the recordkeeper's quarterly statements or the TPA's discrimination testing does not vary based on the size of the participant's account balance. There are recordkeeping contracts that do not provide for per head pricing, but in these situations we derive the per capita (per head) cost so that price comparisons can be made. Secondly, pay for services that achieve measurable results. Mailings, participant advice, allocation services, and website or enrollment gadgets need to show they are effective. Thirdly (as we discuss in detail in the next chapter), screen for low-cost investment management.

Here is our recommended process for plan cost control:

- Establish governance processes to understand fees and expenses and review plan changes.
- Identify all service providers receiving compensation.
- Obtain full fee and expense information.

- Determine what the service providers are being paid.
  - o rates and formulas
  - o actual dollar amounts or estimates
- Verify how the provider is getting paid.
  - o direct compensation
  - o indirect compensation
- Confirm what services are being provided for the compensation being paid.
  - o Are the services necessary?
  - o Are the fees reasonable?
- Obtain fee and expense benchmarking data for your plan size and characteristics.
- Remediate or document reasons for significant cost variances from benchmark data.

What Is Our Target for Total Plan Cost?

The cost benchmarks for your plan are a moving target. In addition to the size and participant account, the plan design complexity, education and participant service needs, and specialized features will impact plan cost. Keep in mind that highly customized or unique plan provisions will narrow the field of providers willing or able to service your plan at competitive rates.

The average total plan cost has declined from 1.50 percent a decade ago to 1.28 percent in 2015, based on a sample survey from the *401k Averages Book* published by www.401ksource.com. We think this is still too high. Competition in the industry is constantly driving down costs and driving up features and services. This is true for all the providers—recordkeepers, mutual funds, and plan advisors. For example, in 2011 a mutual fund giant collaborated with the national recordkeeper and launched a low-cost, open-architecture product for plans from startup to $20 million in assets. For a plan with $5 million in assets and one hundred participants, a low-cost arrangement offers a full service package, including recordkeeping, index mutual funds, and average plan advisory fees at an all-in cost in the range of .50 percent to .60 percent.

In light of fee disclosure and better analytic tools available to plan sponsors, other providers have responded by offering lower-cost options. Plan sponsors have expanded the offering of lower cost and index funds in the plan menu, and the use of revenue-sharing fee credits returned to the plan is now a common practice. Plan sponsors should scrutinize embedded expenses in recordkeeping contracts, annuity and guaranteed interest accounts, and broker/advisor compensation.

Here are our guidelines for market competitive cost structures:

- Passive/Index Investments   0.05-0.20%
- Actively Managed Investments   0.20-0.50%

- Average Blended Investment Menu   0.20-0.40%
- Advisor/Consultant   0.10-0.50%

- Total Variable Expenses   0.30-0.90%
- Plus Fixed Costs of $55-$150 per Balance for Recordkeeper / TPA / Custodian

Manage the Growth of Terminated Accounts

You should monitor your quarterly plan administration reports with an eye toward managing the cash out of terminated participants—in particular, the small accounts under $5,000. This is an IRS compliance issue and an important fiduciary duty. When terminated participants become "lost" due to address changes, fiduciaries have an obligation to use reasonable efforts to locate the lost participant and see that the account balance goes to the correct owner. Your plan document addresses the handling of terminated participants, and the sponsor remains responsible for mandatory age 70 ½ distributions.

Each of these terminated accounts adds to recordkeeping and compliance costs, and, as we remind our clients, the plan sponsor remains the liable fiduciary for these terminated employees who must receive all the same notices and services of active participants. If your plan expenses are paid from plan assets, keep in mind that with per capita pricing (equal quarterly fee per person), at least the terminated participant is paying a fair share. On the other hand, if your plan has asset-based pricing, the average and larger accounts are subsidizing the cost of terminated-plan participants. We also remind plan sponsors the growth of terminated accounts might push the plan participant count over the 120 number. When the number of participants reaches the 120 mark, a plan that previously filed the short 5500 will now be required to file the longer 5500 filing and engage a public accounting firm to conduct an independent plan audit. This audit could cost $7,000–$10,000 or more per year.

Review the cash-out, terminated account procedures with your recordkeeper to ensure the company HR/payroll function is updating the status of participants and providing for distribution of required notices. When assisting plan sponsors in the vendor selection process, we compare recordkeeper capabilities and procedures in this area with an eye toward the optimal level of automation and outsourcing. During plan recordkeeping installation, you can ensure a more seamless cash-out procedure by establishing a periodic and complete update of employee census information. An important solution for small accounts is the deemed IRA. ERISA permits the plan sponsor to transfer small terminated accounts to an IRA, thereby removing the account from the plan.

Making the Transition from Hidden to Transparent Pricing

Many small plans started with group annuity contracts and have had embedded asset-based pricing. The notion of moving to lower-cost transparent pricing sounds attractive, until the human resource manager realizes that the employees will now see plan expenses on their quarterly statements. The impact of this change will depend on the characteristics of the participant population, considering their tenure as participants and their exposure to plan education. The employer may be concerned that employees will not join the plan if they see that there are costs, or they may begin to question the costs. Since the founding of our firm in 1995, we have handled this transition for hundreds of plan sponsors. It is easy and simple to explain, and the participant education underscores for employees the effort the employer has made to control costs on their behalf.

Action Items

- ✓ Review all plan fee disclosure documents and determine total and per capita plan costs for each plan service and vendor.
- ✓ Identify all revenue-sharing sources and arrangements.
- ✓ Benchmark and compare plan services and fees.
- ✓ Determine and document that services provided to their plan are necessary and that the cost of those services is reasonable.
- ✓ Develop a plan expense policy to govern the type and amount of expenses paid by the plan sponsor or from plan assets by per capita or pro rata methods, including the treatment of revenue sharing and recapture.
- ✓ Lower plan costs and fiduciary responsibilities by reducing the growth of terminated accounts.

Chapter 6

Vendor Management
and Benchmarking

B y vendors, we are referring mainly to the recordkeeper and/ or the third-party administrator (TPA) that provides those essential components for your plan, although the process and advice here would apply to other plan services—advisory, audit, legal, custodian/trust, and investment management.

Vendor management is the business process of selection, evaluation, and ongoing monitoring and supervision of plan vendors. It is a key fiduciary task delegated to the person or firm entrusted to act as your plan advisor. So, your plan advisor should be in place before a recordkeeper is evaluated. On occasion, we see the cart before the horse—a recordkeeper is selected, and later the plan sponsor engages an advisor and thereby loses some of the long-term value that the plan advisor would be providing. In almost all plan advisor compensation arrangements, the vendor management process is part of the plan advisor's service package.

Your plan advisor will serve as an intermediary and advocate and provide support and advice throughout the selection process and continuing with all aspects of vendor management.

If you are working with an independent, expert plan advisor, he or she will have specific knowledge and conflict-free access to all the solutions in the marketplace. Some of the most attractive and cost-effective plan providers do not advertise or market directly to plan sponsors, usually because they do not sell retail brokerage, insurance, or investment products to the public. A brand name can be easier to sell to participants or a large board of directors, but a brand name earned from insurance, mutual fund, or brokerage services may or may not translate to good value from that provider's 401(k) subsidiary.

The selection of your plan vendors should also occur after you have considered or consulted on key plan design objectives and policies for your plan. A fully bundled, brand-name provider with proprietary funds may not be compatible with customized plan design and an investment policy statement that presumes open-architecture investment options.

In selecting a 401(k) recordkeeper or TPA, we apply the same business criteria you would use in selecting an important vendor as business partner: business stability and integrity; an independent audit of system controls and operations; service measurements and expectations; financial strength and technology; and staff experience and training capabilities. However, as fiduciaries and in the interest of our fiduciary clients, we start with a preference for low-cost and open-architecture investments. Certain plan features and services are especially valuable and effective: in-depth participant statistics and outcomes reporting; plan level investment allocation models; ERISA consulting and legal assistance; participant-specific and personalized retirement readiness communications.

We want to emphasize that there is no perfect decision or perfect choice—no one size fits all. Vendor selection is a process that should not have a predetermined outcome. Analyze all the available information and let the process reveal the final choice. All the data points will weave together in a tapestry that reveals a prudent selection.

The Competitive Landscape

This is a very competitive industry with a variety of players coming from different organizational and business structures, including insurance, mutual fund, brokerage, and record processing. If, in the last eighteen to twenty-four months, you have not compared and benchmarked your plan with the industry leaders, you may find new services and features and attractive pricing that will benefit your participants. Here we offer a few highlights about the different providers in the industry.

A century before the age of the 401(k), insurance companies essentially invented the retirement plan with the lifetime annuity payment that was the original plan for accumulating and paying income in retirement. Leveraging their resources for agent training and distribution, and reliable systems for servicing policyholders, the insurance companies have focused their market strategy on ease of use, high touch service, and well-integrated processes. The insurance companies pioneered the group annuity contract that provides a streamlined package of 401(k) services—preselected investment menu, guaranteed interest account, recordkeeping, custodian/trustee, participant reporting, and educational materials—with an easy, sign-on-the-dotted-line contract. The group annuity contract may include compliance and administration or may offer those services from a local TPA.

The advantages of the group annuity contract package can also be seen as the disadvantages. Annuity contract compensation and costs are embedded and more difficult to isolate. Moreover, the investment menu selected by the insurance company includes funds that may be proprietary and/or favored for revenue sharing. The contract itself is a very complex insurance policy with termination or market value withdrawal limitations that are not well understood by fiduciaries. In chapter 7 on plan investments, we discuss the complexity and concerns surrounding stable value and insurance company general accounts.

Bank trust operations and brokerage firms have always managed institutional and pension assets, and with the advent of 401(k) plans, they extended their local business and trust account relationships to plan sponsors. They offer familiarity and a dependable brand. Banks act as investment advisors and position themselves as such with plan sponsors. They often maintain recordkeeping operations and have the advantage of open architecture, meaning the plan sponsor can select from thousands of funds. The list may include the bank's proprietary funds. Bank trust departments focus on wealth management for individuals or institutions. We find they usually do not support robust ERISA consulting or participant education. Also, bank trust departments may act as the combined recordkeeper, trustee, and plan advisor, which raises conflicts of interest.

Mutual fund companies with millions of individual investors have expertise in individual account recordkeeping and call centers, which is how they entered the 401(k) business. Fund companies enjoy brand-marketing advantages for investors. They leveraged their account recordkeeping and technology advantages to offer lower costs and high-tech website services. Since their core business is asset management, the mutual funds have a strong tendency to favor their own funds. They are strong on investment expertise but generally weaker on ERISA plan design and compliance delivery.

HR and payroll companies have capabilities in business process outsourcing and offer convenience for employers who utilize their payroll services. They do not sell proprietary funds and often have open-architecture platforms available to small plans. Their business prowess is data management and automation, but they have not invested heavily in the ERISA consulting side of the business.

Often eschewing any direct marketing or advertising, pure recordkeepers are agnostic to the choice of investments, have built platforms dedicated to 401(k) servicing, and maintain a high level of ERISA expertise. They originated the open-architecture approach and usually offer lower costs.

The last ten years have seen the growth and prominence of

the pure independent 401(k) recordkeepers, which can connect with any plan advisor, multiple trust/custodian options, open-architecture investments, and in-house ERISA and compliance specialists or an external TPA. Pure recordkeepers have been the primary agents driving down costs in the industry. In fact, other brand-name financial institutions have contracted with these recordkeepers to provide the underlying processing and services for the 401(k). The advantage to this arrangement is that the brand company (bank, insurance company, or mutual fund) manages the underlying recordkeeper relationship while the plan sponsor has a brand name to present to participants.

Pure recordkeepers do not market or advertise other products directly to plan sponsors or participants, whereas a bank or insurance company has multiple lines of business to cross-sell. The independent recordkeepers are not investment advisors and leave the menu selection to the plan sponsor and their advisors. They are usually the most cost effective, and pricing is transparent with excellent billing flexibility—based on per head costs, per capita or pro rata. A pure recordkeeper can price services without asset-based charges.

Some small plans with twenty or fewer participants still use individual brokerage accounts to recordkeep their plan balance. Individual brokerage accounts were used in an earlier version of open architecture. The broker-dealers themselves are trying to discourage their brokers from using these accounts as retirement plan vehicles because they lack ERISA controls, reporting and DOL disclosure requirements. Most of these plans are in the process of converting to a recordkeeping platform with one of the provider types above.

What to Include in a 401(k) Request for Proposal

We break down vendor selection into these six categories for examination in the request for proposal (RFP) process:

1. **Cost and expense allocation.** This is a component of intense focus by the federal government and the financial

media. It is a critical fiduciary responsibility, and it is the most obvious legal and employee-investor flashpoint. Unlike the recent wave of "excessive fee" lawsuits, we have not seen a serious complaint or lawsuit concerning website features, for example. However, the plan sponsor is not required to choose the lowest-cost provider but is looking for "reasonable" cost in consideration of the services provided.

2. **Investment fund availability, restrictions, and contract penalties.** Our firm looks for an open-architecture investment platform that makes low-cost investment options available. We want to eliminate proprietary requirements and conflicts of interest between the recordkeeping platform and investment choices. A narrow or restricted investment platform will handcuff the investment due diligence work of the plan advisor. We think it is critical to maintain flexibility in a choice of the QDIA (qualified default investment alternative), because of the impact on automatically enrolled employees and the key role this investment choice plays in fiduciary liability. Our first two screens—cost and investment choices—will narrow the number of vendors we would normally consider.

3. **Participant communications and engagement.** Next, we look to the tools and materials available from the recordkeeper to assist the plan advisor with participant education and communication campaigns. Depending on the employee population, we will look for both web-based and hard-copy materials and mailings that will engage participants in the process of education and goal setting. If the number of participants going online is very low, we look for customized communications that are effective in producing participant action.

4. **Service model, staffing, and measurements.** We encounter three common plan sponsor service models in the industry. You should be able to identify each one and

determine if the model offered by the provider meets the needs for your plan. It is also important for comparing value between providers. The shared service team approach provides a toll-free telephone number or group e-mail to a group of plan administrative specialists, and no particular representative is assigned to the plan. This is the economy service model but can be perfectly satisfactory for a small or basic safe harbor 401(k) plan, as long as the representative who answers the call or e-mail can act as a single-point-of-contact so that the plan sponsor call is not put on hold and forwarded on to representatives at other departments. An assigned account executive model is a higher service model. The account executive becomes familiar with specific plan needs and coordinates responses and production with internal departments. A dedicated administrator / dedicated team is the highest service model and is typical for larger participant populations (one thousand or more) and more complex plans. The dedicated administrator/ team is directly performing or overseeing the production of the plan processes and reports. You would expect the dedicated administrator to have detailed knowledge of your plan provisions and processes and be able to customize procedures and reports.

Early ERISA regulations started with two or three notices to distribute. The number of potential disclosures and notices, such as distributions, SPDs, safe harbor, fee disclosure, blackout notices, QDIA, 404(c), and auto enroll, has risen to as high as ten. Employers are looking to outsource this responsibility as much as possible.

5. **Technology and automated features for the plan sponsor and participants.** For the employer, we look for automated distribution and testing, census and payroll updates, and customized loan and eligibility reporting. For participants, we look for an interactive online enrollment and education experience.

6. **Provider integrity and stability** (audited evaluations, disaster and recovery capabilities, financial strength and ownership). With price competition, demands of technology, and high service needs, consolidation is the business trend in the 401(k) industry.

Second- and third-tier providers have been acquired by larger organizations. The remaining small providers struggle to provide services efficiently. However, all plan sizes have access to good pricing and a top-ranked provider that meets all of the standards we would apply.

Ongoing Vendor Management

At the start of each vendor relationship, you should set goals and objectives in a written service plan. Then, track the timing and frequency of each service delivered. Maintain this information in your fiduciary file for future vendor evaluations.

An onsite visit to your recordkeeper during the selection or later for oversight as a fiduciary will be educational and beneficial to the plan and participants. A site visit is an opportunity to tour the facilities, see the processes in place, and meet the personnel. A home office executive can provide insight into company strategy and industry developments. If not practical for the plan sponsor, your plan advisor who is a specialist has already made these visits to the providers. If you have selected an expert plan advisor, they might save you the time and expense of the site visit. It is highly beneficial to develop a home office relationship with a management contact above the assigned account executive. When issues need to be escalated, the plan advisor and plan sponsor know a company official who can intervene or assist by introducing additional or technical resources.

Periodic Benchmarking Analysis

At the heart of your fiduciary responsibility is the requirement to perform and document a thorough market analysis to benchmark the plan provider services, investment options, and total plan fees. This is an essential role and service to be provided by the plan advisor. There are ninety-plus plan providers that we consider worthy of consideration and about 450 data points used to evaluate them. Our firm has access to proprietary data that enables us to evaluate any aspect of a provider's services and capabilities.

Whether you are selecting a new vendor, replacing a current provider, or performing a benchmark analysis, the traditional method for market analysis is to prepare a request for proposal questionnaire and contact at least four and up to eight providers appropriate for your size and type of plan to request a proposal. Ascertain from each vendor their interest in responding to the RFP and basic capabilities with regard to the plan. Your advisory firm should discuss the RFP with each vendor, respond to questions, and update the RFP as needed.

The next step is to collect, clarify, and organize the information from each proposal. Compare your current state to the desired future state or opportunities. If it is worthwhile to resume the process, determine the finalists, and prepare for an in-depth examination of their offering.

We recommend that plan sponsors review individual components of their plan on a yearly basis and perform a full benchmarking analysis with a market survey of competitive bids on a three- to five-year cycle. Significant plan asset growth and significant increases in the average account balance should also trigger a review.

The traditional style of benchmarking is labor intensive and does not yield a data-rich analysis. We have enhanced this process with newer analytic tools that benchmark value received and the reasonableness of fees. It is also important to use independent sources to benchmark the investments and all the plan services, including the plan advisor (or broker) that may be providing the report. Top plan advisors in our industry understand the fiduciary requirements and expect that the plan sponsor will be reviewing their fees and services too.

Your periodic fiduciary review should also include a look at key metrics illustrating the success of your plan in achieving its goals for the company and the participants. Data-rich reports from recordkeepers and vendors such as fiduciary benchmarks can project retirement plan accumulations at retirement age for individual as well as groups of participants and show utilization rates for plan tools and features.

How to Handle a Plan Conversion

According to surveys conducted by industry consultant firm Cogent, in any particular year, about 11 percent of plan sponsors are likely to change recordkeepers. Some of these conversions from one platform to another will be due to acquisitions and consolidation in the industry. If you have had a plan for fifteen or twenty years, you have probably received one of those letters advising that XYZ is taking over your plan services, and "everything will be okay." As a result of that letter, or dissatisfaction with service levels or pricing, or on the basis of a diligent benchmarking process, you may decide it is your fiduciary duty to take your plan out to market to review the options and consider a new recordkeeper.

Should you choose to make a change, there are some costly and embarrassing pitfalls to avoid in a plan conversion. The change to a different recordkeeper or TPA will often entail a new plan document. This is an important aspect of the conversion, which if overlooked can cause serious problems later on. Vendors may be providing a new prototype document that is a fit to their recordkeeping system. Something in your plan document may change. Prudence and due diligence demands a careful, detailed review of nuanced changes to the plan document. Changes in technical definitions could alter employee benefits or impact internal payroll processes or your time and expense to administer the plan. The new recordkeeper or TPA may not be able to administer important plan provisions, and you may not find out until after the conversion. Request a written review of the changes in provisions. The review consultation will be an opportunity to discard unneeded provisions and match language to actual operations. This process will minimize problems in any future IRS audits. On occasion, we have found customized documents can be amended to conform to a prototype document.

The providers will assign the conversion to a dedicated specialist and offer asset transfer and data conversion options. You might be given a choice between an easy quick remittance method and a more detailed, data-rich template. We strongly advise plan sponsors to spend the time and effort up front in the initial data and payroll interface, so that plan administration going forward can utilize the provider's best reporting and automation features. For example, by providing a periodic data feed on all employees, not just active participants, the recordkeeper can make eligibility determinations and perform periodic discrimination testing. Do not shortcut the data setup to speed up the conversion.

Triple Mapping and Re-enrollment

Our default approach is to transition with as little disruption as possible and minimum participant engagement in the conversion mechanics. We want to provide informational communication and have employees focus on their own personal retirement needs. Our usual practice in the past was to conduct employee meetings before the conversion. Now, we are more likely to hold meetings after conversion when the new plan is "live" at the new carrier. Then, we can bring out the education campaign with the new features and tools, and employees can take immediate action on deferral rate changes and asset allocation. Triple mapping refers to the carrier-to-carrier file transfer of each participant's existing deferral rate election, fund asset allocation, and new money investment allocation elections. No action is required of existing participants.

When the investment fund menu remains the same, the new carrier receives file data from the prior recordkeeper and plan sponsor and maps over the participant's existing elections. When the fund menu is new or revised, the prior fund balance is mapped over to the similar, substitute fund. With fund mapping (with all forms and data in perfect order), the assets are liquidated at the prior carrier on day one, transferred on day two, and repurchased for investment at the new carrier on day three. The time may be a day shorter or longer; but the time out of the market is minimal. In some cases, the same fund can be transferred in-kind with no sale or investment repurchase. For those readers who have not participated in a plan conversion, know that the participant, whether they prefer the old fund or not, does not have the right or power to make the decision as to the manner of the conversion.

Time out of the market for one week during a conversion, when funds are sold and not reinvested, is a common concern that creates more fear than we think is warranted. A handful of days over the course of many decades of investment is essentially a random event.

The downside to fund and existing election mapping is that participants may be mapping over their same 401(k) sins: low deferral rate and poor investment allocation decisions. Our preferred approach is re-enrollment. Any participant below an automatic enrollment rate of 5 percent is defaulted to the 5 percent deferral rate. Those with existing rates above 5 percent are mapped to their same deferral rate election. Before the conversion occurs, all participants are given an opportunity to select new investment allocations, or they are defaulted to the QDIA. We find 90 percent of our clients' participants will remain with the QDIA default portfolio. Of course, after the conversion and armed with the new tools from our education meetings, participants can make more educated and assisted choices.

With the re-enrollment conversion process, plan assets are not reinvested immediately and cannot be transferred in-kind. Funds are liquidated but they can only be reinvested after the participant data and defaults are determined. This is usually completed in five to seven business days.

Action Items

- ✓ Conduct ongoing benchmark and comparative analysis of all vendors.
- ✓ Consider per capita low-cost and open-architecture recordkeeping vendors from across the competitive landscape.
- ✓ Use the event of a plan conversion to a new recordkeeper as opportunity to review plan document and operational risks. Outsource additional tasks.
- ✓ Use triple mapping and QDIA re-enrollment to reduce participant anxiety or confusion and improve participant outcomes.
- ✓ Before or after the plan conversion, make a visit to the recordkeeper (or task the plan advisor to do so) to meet senior managers.

Chapter 7

How to Choose the Ideal Plan Investments

> In every single time period and data point tested,
> low-cost funds beat high-cost funds.
>   —Morningstar, August 9, 2010

Your intuition and your common sense about investing are likely to steer you in the wrong direction. Frankly, it is easier for us to tell you this in writing, not in a meeting, because the truth is so counter-intuitive. But there is reason for the omnipresent warning posted on every piece of investment information available to the public. *Past performance is not indicative of future results. As we say to new investors, past performance represents the earnings paid to other clients.*

For just one example out of thousands, we looked back to 1995 when Everhart Advisors was founded. The cover story of *BusinessWeek* magazine, February 5, 1995 touted "The Best Mutual Funds" and explained that the magazine's Mutual Fund Scoreboard was compiled by Morningstar and could "help you plan your investments and monitor just how your funds are faring." The scoreboard detailed information on 885 equity funds. The article highlights the Lindner dividend fund for its high yield and low risk.

A few years later, in 1998, the fund reported that Lindner Dividend "Tops Morningstar National Rankings."

However, by May 4, 1999, the *LA Times* was reporting that based on the short and long-term results, "the fund ranks in the bottom 2% of its category peers, Morningstar figures show. Even on a 10-year and 15-year basis, at least 80% of Dividend's peers have returned more." After years of losses and underperformance, in 2003 the "low-risk" Lindner dividend fund was acquired and merged into another fund.

This theme of the top-rated funds crashing and eventually closing or merging repeats year after year, but investors continue to chase past performance. Selecting funds according to top Morningstar rankings is likely to result in subpar performance. Hence, chasing past performance is not a prudent process for an ERISA fiduciary.

Why Top Funds Fail to Continue

Our reading of the academic literature reveals that it is close to mathematically impossible for a high-cost, high-turnover, actively managed equity mutual fund to outperform the index over long periods on the basis of the manager's ability. Several factors weigh heavily against the fund's ability to repeat above-average performance. Firstly, the fund's initial success attracts many new investors, and the manager struggles to find attractive investments for the new money flooding into the fund. For this reason, fund companies that adopt a prudent stewardship policy may close a fund when it reaches a certain size. Secondly, even a professional and diligent manager cannot produce sufficient returns above the index to overcome excessively high fund costs. Other studies have found that the manager may have been lucky in the first round and cannot repeat the performance. Talented managers retire or leave the fund family. The most famous case of manager turnover was the departure of Peter Lynch from the Fidelity Magellan fund, which never returned to its former glory.

The evidence points in the same direction over any period. The charts below compare the top performing funds versus their index for successive periods from 1981 through 2002. *These comparisons assume a crystal ball scenario in which you correctly choose with perfect foresight the Top 30 funds for your initial investment.* Imagine that in January 1981 you could predict and invest in the funds that would go on to be the Top 30 performers. There are periods when the Top 30 funds go forward to outperform their benchmark index, but they fail to repeat their success in the subsequent period:

Subsequent Performance of Top 30 Funds		
	Average Annual Total Return Jan. 1976 – Dec. 1980	Average Annual Total Return Jan. 1981 – Dec. 2002
Top 30 Funds	34.33%	9.85%
Index	13.95%	12.22%

Subsequent Performance of Top 30 Funds		
	Average Annual Total Return Jan. 1981 – Dec. 1985	Average Annual Total Return Jan. 1986 – Dec. 2002
Top 30 Funds	21.72%	9.71%
Index	14.72%	11.50%

Subsequent Performance of Top 30 Funds		
	Average Annual Total Return Jan. 1986 – Dec. 1990	Average Annual Total Return Jan. 1991 – Dec. 2002
Top 30 Funds	14.91%	10.14%
Index	13.14%	10.82%

Subsequent Performance of Top 30 Funds		
	Average Annual Total Return Jan. 1991 – Dec. 1995	Average Annual Total Return Jan. 1996 – Dec. 2002
Top 30 Funds	28.19%	2.11%
Index	16.57%	6.89%

Subsequent Performance of Top 30 Funds		
	Average Annual Total Return Jan. 1996 – Dec. 2000	Average Annual Total Return Jan. 2001 – Dec. 2002
Top 30 Funds	30.97%	-22.83%
Index	18.35%	-17.15%

Reprinted with permission by the Financial Planning Association, *Journal of Financial Planning*, February 2006, McGuigan, CFP, Thomas P. "The Difficulty of Selecting Superior Mutual Fund Performance." For more information on the Financial Planning Association, please visit www.onefpa.org or call 1-800-322-4237.

Source: Micropal. The S&P Data provided by Standard & Poor's Index Services Group.

Here is a summary of the research to keep in mind each time you reach for that hot new fund idea:

• Eighty percent of active managers have historically underperformed their index.
• Persistency of outperformance has been very rare. When identifying the 20 percent that did outperform their index over a certain period and carrying the research forward, again we find 80 percent of this group underperforming their index over the subsequent period.

- Survivor bias: over five-year periods, approximately 30 percent of funds have been either closed or merged by the end of the period.
- Manager skill: according to Eugene Fama, professor of finance at the University of Chicago Booth School of Business, it is difficult to prove whether actively managed funds that outperform the market do so out of luck or skill. He found that only the top 3 percent of funds could show results based on the manager's skill and not merely chance (Sam Mamudi, "Top Mutual Funds: Luck or Skill? New Study Questions 'Active' Managers," *Wall Street Journal* [December 3, 2009]).

A Role for Active Management

We will recommend our clients spend their money on active investment management where we have found a strong basis to believe active management will add value. Our criticism of actively managed funds is concentrated on funds with high costs and high turnover. Studies have shown that actively managed funds with low costs and high percentage of manager ownership of the fund may produce improved investment outcomes over long periods.

How to Design an Investment Menu

The process of selecting an investment menu begins with the structure, which refers to the number and types of investment offered to employees. Our goal is to create a portfolio that will minimize the overall risk at a certain expected market rate of return by adding diversification. According to modern portfolio theory, if you blend various "risky" investments, the overall risk of the portfolio may be significantly reduced. By risk, we refer to various investment hazards: inflation, bankruptcy, economic cycles, lack of liquidity, price volatility, and changes in yield.

A well-diversified plan menu can be constructed with 18 to

22 investment choices. Each fund selected may have low or high volatility but should be appropriate as a long-term holding for the participant's account. Ideally, we like to see at least one best-in-class fund selected for each of the nine core equity asset classes, so there is less confusion and minimal overlap presented to participants:

Domestic Equity Investment Styles:

Large Cap Growth	Large Cap Blend	Large Cap Value
Mid Cap Growth	Mid Cap Blend	Mid Cap Value
Small Cap Growth	Small Cap Blend	Small Cap Value

Domestic Bond Investment Styles:

High Quality Short Term	Medium Quality Short Term	Low Quality Short Term
High Quality Intermediate Term	Medium Quality Intermediate Term	Low Quality Intermediate Term
High Quality Long Term	Medium Quality Long Term	Low Quality Short Term

Investment menus have changed over time to include more foreign investments, and this reflects the growth of world GDP outside the United States. We often include a foreign equity fund of non-US investments, an emerging markets equity fund, and a global fund that gives the manager leeway to include both foreign and US investments. As real estate investments have become more securitized, real estate mutual funds have become more available and useful in 401(k) menus.

For fixed income, our recommended menu includes both domestic and foreign bond funds. Bond mutual funds have become more diverse and more sophisticated over time with offerings in short-term, high-yield, foreign, and emerging market bonds. We include a global bond fund to add diversification. A cash option may include a money market, a stable value fund, or a guaranteed investment contract, which is our preference in many cases. 403(b) plans may use insurance company guaranteed annuity contracts but are not permitted under the Internal Revenue Code to use a nonregistered stable value or any other collective trust.

Plan menus can stretch even further to include satellite asset classes, such as emerging market debt, commodities, and natural resource and precious metals funds. We rarely recommend these asset classes as the costs may be quite high, and, besides, a well-diversified global stock or bond mutual fund will include direct or indirect investments that own or benefit from some or all of these satellite asset classes.

Investment Selection and Due Diligence

The next step is to choose the particular fund for each asset class. At Everhart Advisors we follow a strict due diligence process that assists plan sponsors in selecting funds and use a scorecard for fund candidates to be considered. Our fund due diligence includes a thorough analysis of the fund through a well-documented process and proven methodology. This is a core fiduciary requirement. We expect good results, but we protect fiduciaries through the process.

We look well beyond the performance numbers to understand how the manager achieved the performance and responded to different market cycles and economic environments. We apply both quantitative and qualitative metrics to the fund's management, investing strategies, and portfolio. Manager tenure, portfolio turnover, and overall costs are factors, as well as technical measurements of style drift, risk-adjusted performance, up/down capture over market cycles, and peer group ranking.

Along with technical factors about the fund that indicate how it achieved its performance, we apply these key screening requirements:

1. Look for top performers over at least ten-year periods of time over various market cycles.

2. The past performance is only relevant if the fund also has low expenses.
3. Look for a high percentage of manager ownership, meaning that the portfolio managers have their own money invested in the fund.

Our scorecard gives a high weighting to low cost, diversification, and long management tenure. All of the 401(k) platforms we recommend allow us to use both low-cost index and actively managed funds. *Our typical menu of twenty funds will have an average total fund expense in the range of .20 percent to .40 percent.*

The Perils of Selecting an Investment Option for Cash

It can be more challenging to choose an option for cash than to select a mutual fund. An investment option for cash is one of the requirements for 404(c) fiduciary liability protection. With our plan sponsor clients, where we work to keep participants well diversified, we find 3 percent to 7 percent of participant account assets are kept in a secure, stable account. The fixed interest allocation may be much higher for participants close to retirement or considering a plan loan or other distribution event.

Money market options include government-insured and commercial money market funds. Since the 2008 recession, the Federal Reserve has forced low interest rates into the banking system. The result is that money market funds have paid near zero interest rates for several years. With even 2 percent inflation, this is a guaranteed loss to the participant's spending power.

Higher guaranteed yields in the historical range of 2 percent to 2.5 percent above money market rates have been available through guaranteed interest contracts. *There are two main types of guaranteed fixed rate accounts: stable value collective trusts and insurance company general accounts.* In both cases, the term "guaranteed" does not mean government insured but instead refers to the contract or annuity policy guarantee. The story is simple to present to participants: these options have a set quarterly or monthly interest rate, a guaranteed balance at all times, and flexibility for a participant to withdraw or exchange funds, sometimes with limits and time restrictions. However, for the plan sponsor these are complex investments with a separate contract and trust provisions. Terminating a contract at the plan level can involve either waiting for periods of up to two years for outgoing transfers, withdrawal penalties, or market value adjustments. These contract terms can be managed, but the plan sponsor should understand how they operate at the time the contract is signed. Generally, both forms of stable value accounts will prohibit or penalize plan sponsor action to initiate a premature withdrawal or transfer from the account.

The stable value collective trust version operates essentially as a mutual fund portfolio that generates interest income and purchases insurance guarantee contracts to insure that the book value of the account can be paid out to individual participants for distributions or investment exchanges, regardless of the market valuation of the underlying investments in the fund. The stable value fund purchases portfolio insurance, referred to as a "wrapper," to guarantee that a participant can withdraw full benefits on their own individual initiative. As a condition of the insurance wrapper, collective trusts may require the plan sponsor to place short-term exchange restrictions or to exclude competing funds from the plan investment menu.

MetLife, New York Life, and Morley are common providers of stable value collective trust funds to 401(k) plans. The guarantee is contractual and depends on the condition of the underlying investments together with the insurance wrapper. The net investment return on the portfolio determines the interest rate paid. Stable value funds are not registered investment company mutual funds; they are collective trusts. A 403(b) plan cannot use a stable fund; it must use a registered investment fund or annuity. In a 403(b) plan, the insurance company general account is the permissible investment for a fixed interest account other than a money market fund.

The insurance company general account (or "group annuity contract") includes a fixed interest option that is funded and maintained within the reserve account that insurance companies use to maintain sufficient assets to pay policy claims. The claims paying ability of the insurance company supports the "guarantee" on the interest account. The general account investment managers will determine the interest rate paid to participants based mainly on the rates and duration of available high-quality corporate and government bonds. They may also consider the anticipated liquidity needs for claims. Insurance company general accounts may establish a series of interest rate buckets for new and old money, thereby matching interest rates to market rates available at the time of the investment.

As we discussed in the earlier chapter on plan pricing, a proprietary guaranteed interest account within a recordkeeping contract may present a conflict of interest and a fiduciary liability where the guaranteed account is used in effect to hide plan expenses or revenue to the recordkeeper. In 2015, a class action lawsuit brought by 401(k) participants against a large insurance company recordkeeper is working its way through the federal courts. The participants allege that the guaranteed account interest rate is artificially low. The suit also claims that insurance company does not properly disclose its compensation derived and expenses deducted from the account. The nature of this claim would apply to all similar general accounts maintained by insurance companies. For the record, the insurance company regards the complaint "as meritless and will vigorously defend against it." Regardless of the outcome of these legal claims, we recommend our plan sponsor clients search for guaranteed interest accounts with a high financial rating and paying a competitive market rate of return.

To underscore the perils of not maintaining an expert process and documented investment and expense policy, a participant lawsuit against a major oil company alleges the inverse: the company should have replaced a low-yielding money market with a higher-yielding stable value fund. Additionally, the suit claims that the revenue sharing arrangement resulted in extra fees for the recordkeeper as the assets grew and that the revenue was not reasonable because no additional services were rendered to the plan.

A plan sponsor can avoid conflict of-interest situations by using an open-architecture platform where multiple guaranteed interest funds are available, and the recordkeeper is not influencing the choice. We think the possibility of higher returns compared to money market funds are worth the additional effort. We conduct due diligence so our plan sponsors can utilize a guaranteed contract that offers higher returns to participants. We also look for contracts that are transferable, so the investment can be transferred to another trust/custodial platform in the event of a change of recordkeepers.

Choosing a Qualified Default Investment Alternative (QDIA)

With the investment menu in place, the investment fiduciary now faces the most challenging task: the selection of the qualified default investment alternative (QDIA). As we discussed in chapter 3, the QDIA is a cornerstone of your fiduciary protection. We share some thoughts on this next step.

The target date fund approach is widely used and accepted and easy to administer. Tell us your date of birth, and we have a single fund for the remainder of your working days. The target date fund series is a good solution for a plan with automatic enrollment in which a high proportion of participants defaulted into their QDIA. We also see some possible target date disadvantages. After all the due diligence conducted to select a best-in-class investment menu, the participant who defaults into the target date fund will not be invested in any of the selected funds. To achieve broad diversification, the target date fund may invest in ten to twenty underlying funds, which may be managed by the same investment company. However, the single fund family that offers the target date fund may not have the best track record in all of the asset classes within the target date portfolio. A popular alternative is the custom target date portfolio that permits a variety of investment managers to focus on specific asset classes within the portfolio.

The target date fund addresses suitable asset allocation based on time horizon but not based on personal risk tolerance. It assumes a higher risk profile for younger employees, and conservative profile for older employees. This may not be true for the individual. For instance, many younger employees in 2008 found out they were not prepared to accept the high volatility assigned to their target date.

We apply the same fund due diligence for target date funds that we use for the rest of the fund lineup. However, we also review what is called the glide path toward the target date, meaning the change over time in the asset allocation to lower percentages of growth investments. So, for example, comparing different target date fund families, we might find anywhere from 40 percent equities to 60 percent equities at age sixty-five, which is quite a difference to the unwary participant.

Vanguard, Fidelity, and T. Rowe Price remain the three largest TDF providers, collectively holding 70 percent of target date mutual fund assets. Vanguard holds the top spot with about 30 percent market share and uses an all-index approach. The index approach delivers diversified low cost management. In a 2015 evaluation of best-in-class retirement plans by *Plan Sponsor* magazine (May 2015), about 50 percent of plans with a target date QDIA used an index approach. The other 50 percent used either an actively management target date series, or custom target date portfolios. A custom target date allows the plan advisor to select the investment managers to be included in the target date portfolio and may also allow a customized glide path and asset allocation. Of course, this depends on the ability and willingness of your recordkeeper to offer customized portfolios.

At Everhart Advisors, our plan sponsor clients often utilize a customized, risk-based model portfolio as the QDIA. Five risk-based model portfolios are constructed from the best-in-class funds we have already selected for the plan, and we use the moderate risk asset allocation model as the QDIA. These portfolios offer asset allocation, the advisor's selection of investment managers, and automatic rebalancing of their portfolio. In this way, the investment advice as to portfolio composition and rebalancing is built in for the participants and relieves them of the need to make fund selections.

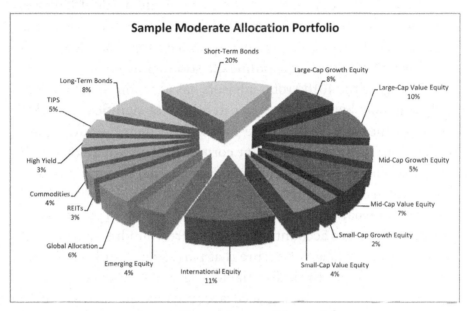

A sample moderate risk model

In our engagement with participants, whether they defaulted or made their own fund selections, we deliver educational presentations and online web-based advice tools to manual participants to select a risk-based model appropriate to their risk tolerance.

Robo-Advised Managed Accounts

As noted earlier, the DOL's regulation for QDIA fiduciary protection specifically included the use of managed accounts as a QDIA. Managed account providers, such as Morningstar, Financial Engines, and Stadion, offer to manage and glide a customized asset allocation for the individual participant, based on the demographics, retirement planning needs and risk tolerance assessment obtained directly from participant input, if any, as well as employer census and plan data. The managed account provider may allocate the account balance to the existing plan menu or introduce its own investment portfolios. Depending on the sophistication of the programming, the service may take into consideration the participant's age and salary, existing retirement account balance, outside retirement and investment savings, desired retirement age, and spousal benefits. They may also update the individual's risk tolerance through periodic online questionnaires.

The age of the 401(k) robo-advisors has been imminent for over a decade now but has failed to catch hold of significant market share as measured by the one meaningful metric—participant utilization. Aside from the giant corporate plans where over half of plans offer the service and individual management is popular with large six- and seven-figure account balances, in the small and midsize plan market, usage ranges around 4 percent of participants. Adding a managed account feature to a three-hundred-participant plan does not indicate or ensure that participants will sign up for the service and pay the individual fee. Several recordkeepers have encouraged the use of managed accounts as the QDIA, which would certainly increase utilization and, by the way, recordkeeping revenue.

As with any investment tool that removes the participant from investment decision making, the managed account providers have marshaled convincing evidence that the service creates net value over costs and better results for managed participants compared to those on their own. However, managed accounts introduce an additional layer of expense (in the usual range of .25 percent to .50 percent, down as low at .10 percent) and face stiff competition from the simpler and less expensive target date fund. We are concerned that the managed account QDIA, applied in the default or re-enrollment scenario, does not meet our fiduciary test: measurable, significant value for the cost. Passive investors who are defaulted to the managed account QDIA are unlikely to make use of online tools for a customized experience.

When Is It Time to Replace or Add an Investment Option?

When evaluating investment options to replace or add to a plan lineup, it is important to have a well thought out investment policy statement to guide fiduciary decisions away from the value-destroying tendencies of human behavior. Our investment policy statement provides a process to evaluate the fund menu by reiterating our selection process.

A few comments are warranted here on the uses and limitations of benchmarks when replacing or adding funds. The components and weighting in an index are constantly shifting and may reflect a portfolio with more or less risk than the investor intends. Most benchmarks are weighted by market capitalization of the component firms. So, companies such as ExxonMobil and Microsoft can represent an oversized share of an index like the S&P 500. In the late 1980s, the MSCI EAFE index for international equity was heavily skewed by unsustainable speculation in Japanese stocks. There are now hundreds of benchmarks available to use for historical return information and to measure investment manager performance. We analyze and select the appropriate benchmark as well as the investment.

In a 2004 study from Emory University entitled "The Selection and Termination of Investment Managers by Plan Sponsors," researchers Amit Goyal and Sunil Wahal found that plan sponsors tend to fire investment managers who then go on to perform better than the newly hired managers. The study looked at 3,600 plans from 1994 to 2003. Likewise, a study by Cambridge Associates LLC for the period 1996 to 2001 found that the fired equity managers surpassed their replacements 60 percent of the time over the next three years. After being fired, the investment managers went on to outperform the benchmark on average by 6.6 percent in the three-year period after the change. These results are attributed to short-term measurement, whereas the investment manager should be measured over a longer term that includes full market cycles.

We suspect there is another factor at work in these unsuccessful changes. The plan sponsor has hired a plan advisor who is trying to create value and justify their fee based mainly on performing investment manager reviews. They have a tendency to make changes more often than the data has shown would be prudent. It is important to consider that the funds that beat their benchmarks over multiple ten-year time frames typically have periods of time where they fall below their benchmark during the period, and regrettably may be kicked out of the menu along the way due to a truncated measurement period.

Issues with Real Estate and Alternatives

Occasionally, a plan sponsor inquires about purchasing land or a building as a plan asset. Promissory notes and gold bars are other investments of interest to some plan sponsors. These are not prohibited by ERISA, and we understand the investment appeal for some. However, real estate and special investments pose significant fiduciary problems, and they are incompatible with a daily valuation recordkeeping platform.

At least annually, the investment must be valued by an independent source so the plan can complete its income and asset statement. When a participant makes a distribution request, the plan administrator must have a way to pay the distribution by liquidating a portion of the special asset or having sufficient cash in the plan to accommodate the distribution request.

Self-Directed Brokerage

A self-directed brokerage option in the 401(k) plan allows the participant to allocate a portion of their account (usually up to 75 percent) to a brokerage platform that allows trading of individual stocks and bonds, ETFs, and mutual funds not available in the core fund menu. This is an add-on feature to the main investment menu. They are not permissible in 403(b) plans. The self-directed brokerage account may have some valuable benefits for more senior employees with larger account balances. Primarily, a participant within reach of retirement can construct a portfolio that provides dividend and interest income and transfer the investments in-kind at distribution, whereas mutual fund holdings on the core platform are liquidated upon distribution. According to a study by Vanguard of its plan population, more than 20 percent of plans with brokerage options are law firms and medical practices. However, less than 1 percent of participants who have a brokerage option in their plan actually use one.

In practice and operation, the brokerage account has not proven to be a fiduciary risk. This might change if the Department of Labor were to suggest or issue adverse regulations. Essentially, these accounts and the investment results are the responsibility of the individual participant.

On the other hand, the fact that the most commonly held investment in brokerage accounts is a mutual fund suggests to us that participants may be duplicating or overlapping investments covered in the core menu. A properly constructed investment menu will include all the diversification with a narrower range of risk.

In our practice, we discourage the use of brokerage accounts within the plan and suggest that participants reserve the use of brokerage accounts for personal assets outside the plan.

A plan can establish fair and reasonable restrictions on the eligibility and use of the account. However, there is one fiduciary issue in particular to guard against. *The plan sponsor must ensure that plan expenses can be fairly allocated to all participants, whether or not they use the self-directed brokerage feature.* We have seen situations where fees were deducted from participant employees in the core menu but not from the owner's brokerage account assets.

Action Items

✓ The investment policy statement (IPS) codifies an expert prudent process, and periodic fiduciary meetings drive the process.

✓ Document investment menu decisions.

✓ Give selection preference and include low-cost fund choices.

✓ Devote significant review time to the selection and monitoring of the QDIA and the cash or stable value fund option.

Chapter 8

Managing for Outcomes and Participant Retirement Readiness

> If you don't know where you are going any road can take you there.
> —Lewis Carroll, *Alice in Wonderland*

I f you are an employer, you want to avoid the situation where an employee cannot afford to retire when the necessary time arrives. And, of course, the situation can be a great worry and disappointment for the aspiring retiree. Retirement readiness is getting employees on the right path and prepared for a comfortable and secure retirement. It is widely accepted by government and academic experts that individuals should prepare a retirement income to replace 60 percent to 80 percent of their final average earnings. This replacement ratio will include social security and all other sources of retirement income from retirement plans and savings, as well as part-time earned income.

The foundation of Everhart's "retirement readiness" strategies is a focus on "controlling the controllable"—participation, deferral levels, and asset allocation. To help plan sponsors manage the plan toward measurable outcomes, we have borrowed heavily from the field of behavioral finance.

We introduce you here to the 90-10-90 goals developed by

Professor Shlomo Benartzi at the Allianz Global Investors Center for Behavioral Finance (See *Save for Tomorrow: Practical Behavioral Finance Solutions to Improve 401(k) Plans* by Shlomo Benartzi with Roger Lewin, 2012) for your plan:

- Ninety percent of eligible employees participate in the plan.
- Ten percent is the average employee deferral rate, not including but assuming that the employer adds a match in the range of 2 percent to 4 percent of annual compensation. This should achieve an 80 percent income replacement including Social Security.
- Ninety percent of participants have a prudent asset allocation for their account, by using a target date fund, plan level risk-based models, or a professionally managed account.

The 90-10-90 objectives may not be realistic for your plan participant population due to workforce demographics or employer cost constraints in maintaining an attractive plan. A benchmark study on plans in your industry can show the features and achievements of successful plans at comparable companies. However, given the current state of retirement savings in the United States, we caution again that the average plan is woefully inadequate. So, the 90-10-90 measurements set a realistic and higher than average goal for your plan. With the right approach, companies with lower paid, younger, and less educated workforces can still achieve remarkable results.

Ninety Percent of Eligible Employees Participate in the Plan

If your plan is now at 40 percent, 50 percent, or 60 percent participation, set an improvement goal over a three-year period and measure the results. Here are several strategies to move the plan's participation rate toward 90 percent:

- Develop an effective and timely communication and education program to show employees the need and value of joining the plan, and in a way that they can envision their success.
- Revise your plan provisions to allow immediate, monthly, or quarterly enrollment.
- Implement automatic enrollment with automatic deferral rate increases and/or simplify the enrollment process.
- If shown advisable by competitive studies, lower the plan pricing and demonstrate transparency so that employees see that the plan provides a good value.
- Simplify the investment process so that employees are not overwhelmed by choices and decisions at the first encounter with the plan.

Ten Percent Savings Rate, Plus Employer Contributions

The education and communication tools should also be geared to encourage employees to increase their savings rate. A 10 percent savings rate of employee contributions is the rule of thumb for most employees. However, the website advice and personalized calculation materials distributed to employees should illustrate their suggested deferral rate (including the employer contribution) to reach their goals. If your plan has automatic enrollment, consider adding the automatic escalation feature, which will increase the employee savings rate by 1 percent a year up to a cap of 10 percent. You can have automatic escalation in the plan without the automatic enrollment feature. Many recordkeepers have technology on the participant website to allow individual employees to set up their own automatic escalation feature when they join the plan.

Another communication tactic borrowed from behavioral studies is to simplify enrollment deferral rate choices. Eliminate deferral rate elections below 4 percent and illustrate contribution elections of 4 percent, 6 percent, 8 percent, 10 percent, and 12 percent percent.

Employees may also be stymied by the thought or disclosure that the plan has costs. Again, we favor simple and full disclosure of expenses. If the pricing and fund menu is structured correctly, the plan will be very attractive to employees compared to outside investment alternatives.

Ninety Percent of Participants Use Automated Investment Allocation

It is a common finding: the funds show a sterling performance report, but the participant results ... not so good. According to the DALBAR Company, for the thirty years ended December 31, 2015, the S&P 500 index produced an annual return of 10.35 percent, while the average equity mutual fund investor earned only 3.66 percent. Investment fund performance is not highly correlated with participant performance. DALBAR reports that the leading causes of the performance deficit are the investment psychology and behaviors that influence all of us. In fact, the inventor of the modern portfolio theory, Professor Harry Markowitz, admitted that emotions of fear and greed affected his own investment choices. We can be successful investors by following a process that eliminates or minimizes our own poorly timed and harmful interventions.

According to a study by the Aon Hewitt actuarial consulting firm and the advice technology firm of Financial Engines, participants invested in a fund, model, or managed account with automatic asset allocation and rebalancing had 3.32 percent higher annual returns net of fees than the do-it-yourself participants. This is a huge differential, and the positive effect was found in every age and grouping. For a forty-five-year-old participant, the built-in advice of an asset allocation model or managed account could translate to 79 percent more wealth at age sixty-five.

Your goal as a plan sponsor should be to have 90 percent or

more of the participants utilizing an automated asset allocation program that handles three critical tasks for participants:

1. Selects and maintains a risk-based allocation between stock, bond, and cash investments
2. Selects funds and asset classes
3. Performs the buy/sell transactions to rebalance the portfolio to the risk-based allocation

A series of target date portfolios or risk-based asset allocation portfolios can serve this purpose very well for almost all plan investors.

Keys to Effective Education and Communications

The 401(k) plan education programs are a lot like our public education for school-age children: everyone gets one, but that does not tell us much about the results. Retirement plan sponsors or their financial advisors spend a considerable amount of time drafting participant communications or conducting presentations in an attempt to increase the number of plan participants, maximize employee deferrals, increase investment diversification, or improve plan metrics. However, the generic approach in these education campaigns is likely to fail. Is it a surprise to you that participants do not read retirement plan communications? A recent study by the International Foundation of Employee Benefit Plans confirmed the obvious, that most participants do not read—or even open—any employee benefit communications sent to them. Even if employees read the communication, the information presented does not lead them to take action. The typical participant communication pieces contain too many charts, too much text, or try to teach financial literacy. If you have ever handed over your car keys to a teenage daughter on a Saturday night, see if she wants to read the manual first. They want to get somewhere; they do not care how it works.

Education and communication will be effective when it is

regular and personalized. A semiannual workshop introduces employees to different topics appropriate to their situation and should provide the opportunity for individual meetings where each participant can develop personal retirement goals. Web-based, e-mail, or hard-copy communications should present information specific to the employee, such as their projected accumulation and income at retirement age, current and projected compensation, and suggested deferral rates. Provide a personalized illustration to each eligible employee showing a paycheck analysis with the net effect on take-home pay at various contribution rates. By providing all the tools and information at the point-of-sale, our prospective 401(k) participant is more inclined to make the decision.

Reinforce the message and provide positive feedback by showing employees their progress over time. Behavioral psychologists believe participants tend to view and treat their future sixty-five-year-old self as if they were dealing with a stranger, and they are not highly motivated to take care of that stranger's retirement. We try to evoke for participants a retirement plan that envisions the future lifestyle and comfort of that stranger-self as well as their future account balance.

Target personalized messages to the appropriate audience. Employees in range of retirement—ten years or fewer—will appreciate a "gap analysis" that estimates any shortfall in annual retirement income including Social Security, based on their current and projected salary, account balance, and investment earnings. For employees who are participating at a low savings rate below the matching cap, they will respond to a message that illustrates the take-home pay cost and annual accumulation of increasing their savings rate to the maximum match cap. If the plan does not use automatic enrollment, try an easy postcard type of enrollment form that minimizes study effort to get started.

Education is just as critical when you have automatic enrollment. When exposed to impactful information and education, many employees will choose a savings rate above the default rate. As we mentioned before, if your automatic enrollment provision starts at a small 3 percent, the hold of inertia may keep the employee contributing at that inadequate level for many years. Worse yet, those same employees are more likely to drop out of the plan than the employees who join on a voluntary basis.

Paralysis by Analysis

A plan investment menu too large, complex, and confusing will inhibit plan enrollment. Studies show that participation starts to decline as the investment menu exceeds eighteen investment options. Holding the weighty sixty-page enrollment book of fund fact sheets, employees see too many investment choices and put off the enrollment until they have time for further study. An investment menu with twenty or more funds can be simplified by offering five preallocated risk models. These well-diversified models are greatly appreciated by the participants to simplify their investment decisions.

Investment education will be useful when it is focused less on how to select and evaluate specific mutual funds and more on successful investment behaviors and perspectives.

Three Participant Investor Profiles: Passive, Engaged, Active

A target date fund is a good choice for the default or passive investor. According to a 2011 study by JP Morgan Retirement Services, 69 percent of participants identify themselves as passive investors, although their investment selections do not match their stated preference. Only 18 percent of their assets are in an asset allocation program. The engaged investor values professional oversight and advice while maintaining control over decisions. The engaged investor is moving up the learning curve and is willing and able to absorb and use some of the education and advice tools. With guidance, the engaged investors will select their own choice of risk-based asset allocation portfolio or use a web-based managed account. The JP Morgan study found 30 percent of participants fit the engaged investor category. The active investor is among the 1 percent of do-it-yourselfers who may use the online advice tools to construct their own portfolio with the personal rebalancing tool.

Agenda of the Employee Group Meeting

We consult with our plan sponsors on the purposes to be achieved at employee group meetings. We recognize that this is an employee relations event. You want employees to appreciate the time, money, and effort the company has expended on the plan and to know that the company wants to help employees achieve retirement readiness.

The presentations and material used at the meeting should be geared toward education on topics that employees need to know *to take action on items they can control*: determining their desired income need and required retirement accumulation amount, determining a savings rate, understanding their personal time horizon and risk profile, and choosing an asset allocation. The meeting should include an explanation of key plan document provisions and available participant services and technology. The meeting is a good occasion to introduce web-based tools.

If the plan has changed provisions or vendors, the meeting should include a brief explanation of the reasons for the change, the fiduciary process, and the internal and external leaders and advisors participating in the process. Employees may be skeptical of plan changes and assume that the employer was seeking an advantage to the company. Remind participants of the employer's fiduciary duty and explain advantages that both the company and employees should expect.

Our purpose is not to turn employees into investment experts, and, in our view, time spent reviewing mutual fund portfolios or explaining alpha and beta fund measures is not useful. The group meeting is not a good forum for an individual investor to master the market behavior of high-yield funds in a rising rate environment, or value versus growth investment styles. That type of information is better suited for a one-on-one session, which should be offered by your advisory firm as well.

Employers are becoming more interested in employee financial wellness beyond the 401(k) plan. To meet this need, our firm recently introduced semiannual "after-hours" participant workshops covering varied topics, with invitations to all client employees and their spouses. The topics have included social security optimization, understanding Medicare and health care costs in retirement, and others. This is an education resource that has been very well received by our clients and impactful for employees.

Instant Change: The QDIA Re-enrollment Strategy

Most plans are well below the 90-10-90 targets. Employee participation, savings rates, and asset allocation are not on the path to success. The plan can remedy these problems in one thorough process. It is called a "QDIA re-enrollment" and involves a refresh for all participants, giving them an opportunity to review and learn about current plan features and investment options and make new elections. Earlier, we introduced re-enrollment in connection with a plan conversion. A plan conversion and change of recordkeepers is an opportune time for re-enrollment, but it can be done at any time chosen by the plan sponsor.

Of course, the plan should already have the desired plan design, features, and pricing in place. Education meetings are conducted. Automatic enrollment is implemented for employees not enrolled in the plan. In addition, participants are moved from their current investments and defaulted into a qualified default investment alternative (QDIA) target date fund or asset allocation model, unless they make an affirmative election during the re-enrollment timeframe, which may be a fifteen- to thirty-day window. Employees who take their own account action during the re-enrollment window are not moved into the QDIA default investment. Likewise, employees who affirmatively elect a contribution percentage are not automatically enrolled at the default rate of contribution.

We have seen spectacular success with re-enrollment, including significant improvements in savings rates and in participant asset allocation/investment diversification. Moreover, the plan sponsor gains the fiduciary protection of the QDIA process.

As the plan administrator and fiduciary, the plan sponsor has the authority under ERISA to implement the re-enrollment. Moreover, the process will enhance the plan sponsor's fiduciary protection. If the plan has participants who have been defaulted to a money market or a non-QDIA default investment in the past, the re-enrollment will move their funds to the QDIA, thereby affording fiduciary coverage to the plan sponsor on that account. When the re-enrollment involves automatic enrollment, a change in investment menu and a blackout period longer than three days, employees receive the required thirty-day notices.

Here is a recommended project plan for the re-enrollment:

Sixty-Days-Prior Announcement (E-mail or Flyer)
- informs participants of upcoming re-enrollment
- provides information on what to expect and key dates

Thirty-Days-Prior Notice and Enrollment Material
- provides required notification language and blackout dates, if applicable
- highlights available investment options
- provides opt-out process for choosing investment elections for participants who do not want default investments

Seven-Days-Prior Education Meetings and Final Reminder
- Conduct education meetings to reinforce key messages.
- Send final reminder informing participants of the re-enrollment window dates.

Two- or Three-Week Re-enrollment Window
- During this time period, participants have the option to elect a deferral rate and select investments other than the QDIA.

Re-enrollment Window Closes

Participants without an affirmative election are enrolled at the automatic enrollment savings rate. Participants without an investment election will have assets defaulted into a QDIA. What can you expect from this strategy? We find that the active and engaged participants who make elections during the window period will likely increase their deferral rates and improve their investment allocations, and the less interested and more passive investors will follow the implicit advice of the program.

How Important Is Fund Selection for Participants?

What is the importance of fund selection in participant outcomes? Every plan and investment advisor has some or great expertise and tools for fund evaluation, and many fiduciaries dedicate a large amount of their focus to selection and replacement of funds in the investment menu. Frankly, investment advisors have a natural tendency to emphasize those areas of specialized knowledge that is most in demand and marketable in their wealth management practices. The attention and effort by fiduciaries to examine funds finds its way into communication and education programs for participants.

At your next fiduciary meeting, you should look at the agenda. Many committees could spend less time on the choice of a substitute large cap value fund, for example, and more time on participant results. A study by Putnam Investments using thirty years of data (W. Van Harlow, PhD, CFA, "Defined contribution plans: Missing the forest for the trees?" PutnamInstitute.com, May 2014) and our own experience demonstrates that fund selection is a factor in participant outcomes but it is clearly less impactful to participant outcomes than deferral rate decisions and asset allocation. Fund due diligence is an important fiduciary duty, but the real impact on participant outcomes suggests that fiduciaries and participants should focus on the elements where they have the most control: savings rates and asset allocation.

There is another 90 percent rule to keep in mind: asset allocation determines more than 90 percent of a participant's investment return. So, the performance difference, for example, between one large cap fund compared to a substitute is far less significant than the choice of what percentage of an account is maintained in that asset class. Secondly, a 1 percent increase in deferral rate in a plan with bottom-quartile investment performers will far outgrow a 1 percent lower savings rate in a plan with crystal ball accuracy of always choosing top quartile performers.

Action Items

- ✓ Devote more time and resources as a fiduciary to "controlling the controllable" 90-10-90 goals and less time on individual investment fund selection.
- ✓ Aim for 90 percent participation rates, 10 percent deferral rates, and 90 percent appropriate asset allocation.
- ✓ Focus participant education on investment and savings behavior and away from specialized investment information.
- ✓ Use QDIA re-enrollment to reset participants with an appropriate investment allocation and minimize fiduciary risks.

Chapter 9

Four Success Stories

W e have a passion for this business, and we have had a few words to say about it. There is nothing theoretical about *The 401(k) Owner's Manual*. We share our processes and recommendations because we have seen the results repeatedly. Here are several success stories from our plan sponsor clients who wanted to address shortfalls and make improvements to their plans.

Overcoming Apathy and Mistrust at an Industrial Company

Plan Conditions: A small industrial company with a blue-collar workforce sponsors a 401(k) plan with a very generous 100 percent matching contribution up to 7 percent of annual compensation. Despite the time, money, and effort the company had put into offering the plan, 58 percent of eligible workers were not enrolled and were leaving behind a huge benefit over a long period. The company was concerned about the future financial security of these employees and bewildered by the lack of response. What were these eligible employees thinking? We found a range of responses. The employees were overwhelmed and intimidated by the concepts, written notices, and material from the plan. There was general skepticism and mistrust by employees. Some thought there must be a catch and the offer might be too good to be true. Other employees were just living by paycheck with no thought of the future, and no one associated with the plan had challenged them to consider their future.

Solutions: First, we brought in the right tools to get individual employee attention. Considering the demographics of the targeted group, we used a "gap analysis" communication and distributed a personalized report to each eligible employee. The report took into account their age and salary, estimated social security, and projected their retirement income needs at age sixty-five, compared to their current state. The calculations also provided each employee with a recommended contribution rate to close the gap. We conducted small group meetings in a casual setting, focused their thinking on the future, showed how the plan could help, and explained some basic arithmetic along with net versus gross pay and tax benefits. We then met with each "eligible employee not participating" on a one-on-one basis, provided further retirement needs analysis, and fine-tuned their individual calculations to include spousal information.

Results: Within one year, we were able to increase the participation rate to 84 percent. Every employee who participated in an individual meeting enrolled in the plan.

Fiduciary Fear in the C-Suite

Plan Conditions: A construction services firm is a public company with three thousand employees and has a full HR group with resources dedicated to the plan. They were working with a national brokerage firm as the plan advisor. However, the company was lacking a fiduciary governance function and was facing an upcoming Department of Labor examination. Executives were worried about their fiduciary responsibilities. When we were engaged to review the plan, one executive asked, "Would it make sense to shut the plan down?"

The company had received the vendor fee disclosure, but the opaque pricing structure and abstruse terminology inhibited understanding of plan costs. They were unable to fulfill their fiduciary duty to determine if the individual cost components of the plan were reasonable, mainly because they could not decipher the underlying revenue sharing arrangements. The company also needed assistance in benchmarking their plan costs and services to plans of similar participant count, asset size, and complexity. This was complicated further by the fact that their national provider was serving in both the advisor and recordkeeping roles.

Solutions: We interpreted the fee disclosure, determined the total and component costs, and then benchmarked the plan. The company had only identified about $10,000 of direct costs. Through a review of all contracts, trust statements, and mutual fund data, we uncovered additional indirect asset-based compensation of $110,000 received by the recordkeeper from investment funds within the plan. Adding all sources of direct and indirect compensation, we determined that the plan cost for recordkeeping was equal to $130 per participant account balance. Utilizing quotes from top-tier vendors, we negotiated the expense down to $87 (fixed fee) per balance.

The company established fiduciary governance procedures that included a fiduciary committee with a charter and investment policy statement. They began quarterly meetings, continuing documentation, and a due diligence process for investments. To prepare for the DOL examination, we walked through a forty-point compliance checklist and conducted fiduciary education.

Results: The recordkeeper established a revenue-sharing account to recapture asset-based revenue. Plan expenses decreased by 35 percent, with most of this savings resulting from the recapture of revenue sharing on behalf of participants. The fee structure changed from variable to fixed recordkeeping costs, so the plan sponsor could more easily determine that expenses were reasonable. The fiduciaries feel assured that the plan has a sound governance program. There were no significant issues from the DOL examination.

Set It, Forget It, and Neglect It

Plan Conditions: This high-profile company has a national name-brand product and is located in a small Midwestern town where it is the largest employer. Since the Great Recession of 2008–2009, the loyal workforce has been preoccupied with declining revenues and the future of the business. It is a difficult time at the company, including changes in leadership and attrition. A longtime core workforce remains. The plan has over four hundred participants and $20 million in assets. Participants have neglected their individual asset allocations.

The advisor to the plan conducted fiduciary meetings that focused on the review and selection of plan funds. Employees were enrolled but not engaged with the plan. Most participants had selected a few mutual funds or defaulted to the money market at the time they enrolled and never made a change to their initial selection. Over time, the plan investments and participant risk were misallocated: younger participants were still in the money market, and older participants were over weighted in equities. Inertia ruled the day.

The company was worried in particular about the employees age sixty-two and older. Of that group, only 6 percent had their investments properly allocated. Many of these longtime employees had not revised their investment choices since the time they first enrolled in the plan. A sharp or prolonged market decline could devastate their retirement planning.

They tried to remedy the problem by adding more funds. This had an even worse effect as some participants assumed that the addition of new funds was a message that they should abandon other investments. Increasing the size of the menu also led to paralysis by analysis.

Solutions: The company decided to implement a QDIA (qualified default investment alternative) re-enrollment process as we described in chapter 8. The company advised all participants that as of an announced date, their current account balances and future contributions would be invested in the plan's QDIA, unless participants opt out by making their own investment selections by a predetermined date before the re-enrollment.

We assisted the plan sponsor with the selection of a target date fund series as the QDIA and selected a best fit according to the plan demographics. We followed up the program with education and employee engagement.

Results: The table below shows the before and after results of the QDIA re-enrollment process:

	Before Re-enrollment	After Re-enrollment
% Participants under-exposed to equity	28%	2%
% Participants over-exposed to equity	59%	2%
% Assets in Target Date Funds	22%	93%
% Participants in any TDF	68%	98%
% Participants with 100% of assets in Target Date Funds	13%	96%

Re-enrollment facilitated a major correction in asset allocation throughout the plan, redirected new money contributions, and put 93 percent of assets under ongoing management and reallocation.

Older participants adjusted their exposure to equity to an appropriate risk level. Younger participants increased utilization of target date funds, which improved the ongoing balance and reallocation of their accounts with the appropriate growth component. Re-enrollment also eliminated fiduciary risk from participants who in the past had been defaulted to a non-QDIA investment option.

Tip of the Iceberg: Owners Learn What Lies Below

Plan Conditions: A medical instrument distributor sponsors a safe harbor 401(k) profit-sharing plan with thirty participants, annual contributions of $1 million, and $12 million in assets. With an average account balance at a rich $400,000, this plum account was enriching the vendors but not offering reasonable value to the participants or to the three owners, whose accounts equal about $3 million of the plan's assets. The plan was priced with variable asset-based fees and was steering toward a *Titanic* fiduciary iceberg. Unseen costs were growing every year and reached a point where the recordkeeping and TPA costs were nine times the comparable market rate. If left alone, the lack of cost control was going to cost the participants an unnecessary $600,000 over the next ten years. Moreover, the investment menu had several funds that warranted removal or watch list status due to poor historical performance or qualitative factors. Cost improvements were also available in the investment menu as well.

The plan advisor was receiving reasonable annual compensation of .20 percent. However, ERISA requires that the compensation must be reasonable for the services provided, and this advisor's service package was lacking key components for the fee received. In addition to the problems noted above, we learned the owners were unaware of a huge opportunity to reduce their current income taxes.

Solutions: Cost control is one of the key tasks of a plan advisor. We compared current plan recordkeeping costs to six other providers and found a top-tier provider that offered a fixed annual recordkeeping fee instead of the asset-based fee. We benchmarked the advisor fee and recommended an appropriate schedule of plan advisory services commensurate with plan characteristics and plan sponsor needs.

The plan advisor and other vendors had overlooked valuable plan design alternatives and underutilized tax benefits. Looking at business profitability, plan data, and demographics, we observed that a combination cash balance and 401(k) profit-sharing arrangement might provide extraordinary benefits to the owners. Three key factors supported the feasibility of a cash balance plan: 1) the successful business enjoyed steady cash flow and profits, 2) the owners ranged in age from forty-five to fifty-two with younger employees, and 3) the existing plan was already providing non-highly-compensated employees with a generous employer safe-harbor and profit-sharing contribution in the range of 7 percent of annual compensation. We engaged an actuarial consultant to provide a cost-benefit study for a new plan design with the objective of determining the maximum additional benefits to the owners without a cost increase in contributions to employees.

Results: The cost and plan design calculations were astounding to the owners, who were both relieved by the results and chagrined at their past inattentiveness to the plan. A new top-ranked recordkeeper with an open-architecture platform offered an annual fixed fee of $4,175 based on the number of account balances, instead of the prior asset-based fee equaling $39,440. Projected over ten years, the savings would amount to $603,840. We were also able to make improvements to the fund menu.

The company implemented a new combination cash balance and 401(k) profit-sharing design. In addition to the three owners, the company selected three more key employees to receive enhanced benefits. Altogether, the six key participants were able to receive an additional annual tax deductible (to the business) and tax-sheltered (to the participants) contribution for $809,000, on top of the $324,000 in contributions that were already available and utilized in the prior 401(k) profit-sharing plan. Moreover, the new design did not cut back employee benefits or increase employee costs.

Conclusion
Key Best Practices

In conclusion, we summarize key points on how to establish and maintain an optimal 401(k) plan that achieves company goals, protects fiduciaries, and gives participants the best chance to succeed. These recommendations apply likewise to an ERISA 403(b) plan.

- Hire a bona fide plan advisor whose practice specializes in 401(k) retirement plans and can provide objective advice about investment options and plan providers as an ERISA fiduciary. Plan advisory fees and services are negotiable and should be committed to a written agreement.
- Optimize fiduciary protections by utilizing ERISA 404(c), qualified default investment alternatives, and a corporate trustee.
- Identify the fiduciaries to your plan, establish a 401(k) plan committee, and document the process and rationale of fiduciary decisions. Conduct regular meetings for oversight of key plan administration tasks: assure that the plan document is updated and provisions of the plan document are followed; assure that filings and notices are completed; assure that census and payroll functions operate correctly; assure that compliance and discrimination tests

are conducted properly; utilize a benchmarking process to review and determine that plan provider fees are reasonable.

- Terminated participants continue to be the responsibility of the plan fiduciaries and may add plan costs that burden the active employee participants. Actively manage the cash-out of small accounts. This may also help some employers to avoid the 120-participant count that triggers an annual audit.

- Revisit your plan goals and objectives and conduct a thorough review to conform your plan document to your desired plan outcomes. Remove overly complex or underutilized provisions that provide little benefit.

- For higher participation, eliminate roadblocks to enrollment and overcome inertia. Implement all or part of the provisions for automatic enrollment and automatic escalation at a meaningful benefit level. Maximize the impact of employer matching contributions by stretching the match to encourage higher deferral percentages.

- Aim for the 90-10-90 standard: 90 percent participation at 10 percent savings rate with 90 percent of participants in an asset allocation fund or portfolio.

- Retirement-outcomes focused education helps employees envision their retirement readiness. Communications are personalized for participants and provide detailed projections.

- Maintain a useful investment policy statement that documents the prudent process for investment selection and ongoing monitoring and evaluation. Add an expense policy section or addendum that addresses revenue sharing and the selection of fund share classes. Decide on a policy for expense allocation between the plan sponsor and plan assets, and among participants.

- Past performance really does not indicate future results. The ideal investment menu of eighteen to twenty-two funds has one or two best-in-class investment choices in every asset class from low-cost mutual fund companies. Avoid high-cost funds with high portfolio turnover. A low-cost fund menu with both passive and actively managed funds will average between .20 percent and .40 percent expense.

- Focus particular time and effort on the selection of the QDIA, which is where a majority of participants are likely to be invested.
- With careful analysis of provider credit worthiness and contract terms, the plan can select and offer a stable value (insurance company general account for a 403(b) plan) fixed interest option and earn returns that are historically 2 percent to 2.5 percent higher than money market rates.
- Let the plan goals and objectives and the RFP process drive the results of vendor selection without regard to preconceived notions or the marketing budget of the candidates.
- An open-architecture recordkeeping platform without proprietary fund requirements offers the most investment flexibility and avoids conflict of interest issues that could embroil fiduciaries in questionable practices.
- Find all the sources of expense, revenue sharing, and compensation for each component of the plan and determine if each one is reasonable for the service provided. The DOL does not require the lowest-cost fund or provider, but the fiduciary should be confident that the higher-cost option provides a needed or valued service.

How does your plan measure up?

About the Authors

 **Scott Everhart, CFP, AIF** is the president and founding firm member of Everhart Advisors. Scott has specialized in the retirement plan market since entering the financial planning field in 1991, with extensive experience in plan design, investment due diligence, participant education, and fiduciary liability protection. Scott is a nationally recognized advisor and speaks with authority on the topics of fee transparency, revenue sharing, and cost control.

Scott has been named as one of the nation's "300 Most Influential Advisors in Defined Contribution" by 401kWire.com, and "20 Rising Stars of Retirement Plan Advisors" by Institutional Investor News. Scott was honored as one of ten executive "Superstars" by Columbus CEO. Scott has been a guest lecturer at workshops presented with the US Department of Labor and conferences hosted by the Center for Due Diligence, Ohio Society of CPAs, Ohio State Bar Association, Columbus Bar Association, and others.

Scott earned his Certified Financial Planner designation in 1998 and is an Accredited Investment Fiduciary, illustrating knowledge and competency in the area of fiduciary studies. Scott received a bachelor of science degree, magna cum laude, from Kent State University, with degrees in both finance and business management.

He is a member of the Financial Planning Association (FPA), Financial Executives International (FEI), and the Entrepreneurs' Organization-Columbus.

Brian Hanna, AIF is a senior plan consultant for Everhart Advisors. Brian joined the firm in 1997. His focus is on monitoring and increasing retirement plan service levels by acting as an ongoing intermediary between plan sponsors and their respective plan vendors. Brian has received formal training in fiduciary responsibility and due diligence and has extensive experience in plan design, investment selection, and cost control.

Brian has been a guest lecturer at workshops presented with the US Department of Labor, Ohio Society of CPAs, Columbus Bar Association, and the Center for Due Diligence. He has contributed to numerous articles for local newspapers and other publications and was honored by Columbus Business First as a member of the "Forty Under 40" class in 2012. Brian received a bachelor of science degree, summa cum laude, from the Max M. Fisher College of Business at The Ohio State University, with a specialization in finance. He earned the Accredited Investment Fiduciary (AIF) professional designation, awarded by the Center for Fiduciary Studies, in 2008.

Brian currently volunteers as a coach for the Miracle League of Central Ohio, along with leading a bible study at Whetstone Gardens & Care Center. Brian has also participated in missions to Mexico and Honduras, serving and ministering to those in need, along with assisting with the building of schools and homes.

Robert Shwab, CEBS is an independent plan consultant and served as research director for *The 401(k) Owner's Manual.* Rob has thirty years of industry expertise in the design, administration, and sale of retirement plans. Rob started his career with Mutual of America, where he managed a regional retirement plan sales, consulting and service center. He then managed complex plan consulting, risk management, and vendor selection engagements as a senior manager, Retirement Plan Solutions at Ernst & Young. Recently, he served as the regional vice president for Ascensus, one of the largest, independent open-architecture recordkeepers of participant-directed retirement plans. Prior to joining Ascensus, he led client services and business development for the law and TPA firm of MandMarblestone.

He has a BA from SUNY, Purchase and a master's industrial labor relations degree from Cornell University. He earned the Certified Employee Benefit Specialist (CEBS) Fellow designation from the Wharton School and International Foundation of Employee Benefit Plans, and the Accredited Retirement Plan Consultant (ARPC) designation from the Society of Professional Administrators and Recordkeepers. He serves as an industry representative on the FINRA Board of Arbitrators.

Bibliography and References

401k Averages Book. www.401ksource.com.

Aon Hewitt and Financial Engines. "Financial Engines' Help in Defined Contribution Plans: 2006 through 2012." May 2014. https://corp.financialengines.com/employers/FinancialEngines-2014-Help-Report.pdf.

Benartzi, Shlomo, with Roger Lewin. *Save for Tomorrow: Practical Behavioral Finance Solutions to Improve 401(k) Plans.* Allianz Global Investors Capital. 2012.

"The Best Mutual Funds." *BusinessWeek*, February 5, 1995.

Butrica, Barbara A., and Nadia S. Karamchev. "The Relationship between Automatic Enrollment and DC Plan Contributions: Evidence from a National Survey of Older Workers." White paper by Center for Retirement Research at Boston College. July 2015. http://crr.bc.edu.

Dalbar. "22nd Edition of DALBAR's Quantitative Analysis of Investor Behavior (QAIB)." 2016.

Department of Labor. "Target Date Retirement Funds—Tips for ERISA Plan Fiduciaries." February 2013. www.dol.gov/ebsa.

Department of Labor. "A Look at 401(k) Fees." August 2013. www.dol.gov/ebsa.

Goyal, Amit, and Sunil Wahal. "The Selection and Termination of Investment Managers by Plan Sponsors." *The Journal of Finance* 63, no. 4 (August 2008) http://www.hec.unil.ch/agoyal/docs/HireFire_JoF.pdf.

Hutcheson, Mathew D. "Uncovering and Understanding Hidden Fees in Qualified Retirement Plans 3rd Edition." *University of Illinois Elder Law Journal* (Fall 2007).

Investment Company Institute. www.ici.org.

JP Morgan Asset Management. "Understanding Re-enrollment, Benefits for Plan Sponsors and Participants." 2013.

Lim, Paul J. "Lindner Dividend Is Struggling to Regain Its Winning Ways." *Los Angeles Times*, May 4, 1999.

Loesel, Lisa K., and Mark K. Samsa. "View From McDermott: Is *Tibble* the End of Revenue Sharing?" *Pension and Benefits Daily*. Bureau of National Affairs. March 22, 2016.

Malkiel, Burton Gordon. *A Random Walk Down Wall Street: The Time-Tested Strategy for Successful Investing*. New York: W.W. Norton, 2003.

Mamudi, Sam. "Top Mutual Funds: Luck or Skill? New Study Questions 'Active' Managers." *Wall Street Journal*, December 3, 2009.

McGuigan, CFP, Thomas P. "The Difficulty of Selecting Superior Mutual Fund Performance." *Journal of Financial Planning* (June 7, 2006).

Micropal. The S&P Data provided by Standard & Poor's Index Services Group. *Plan Sponsor,* May 2015.

Pool, Veronika Krepely, Clemens Sialm, and Irina Stefanescu. "It Pays to Set the Menu: Mutual Fund Investment Options in 401(k) Plans." *The Journal of Finance* (August 14, 2015).

Principal Group. "Pursuing 'Retirement Plan Success' during Participants' Accumulation Years." April 2010.

State Street Global Advisors. "How to Invest Your Portfolio Using Passive and Active Management." 2011.

Umstead, Dave, and Jim Jasinki. "The Mutual Fund Marketplace Is Broken. Time to Fix It." *Investment News.* June 28, 2015. www.investmentnews.com.

Vanguard. Vanguard Center for Retirement Research. "How America Saves 2015." 2015.

Vanguard. "Vanguard Retirement Plan Access 2015, Industry Benchmark Data Supplement to *How America Saves.*" 2015.

Van Harlow, W. "Defined Contribution Plans: Missing the Forest for the Trees." Putnam Institute Research. May 2014.